How to coach
TABLE TENNIS

David Hewitt

WILLOW BOOKS

Willow Books
William Collins Sons & Co Ltd
London • Glasgow • Sydney • Auckland
Toronto • Johannesburg

First published 1990

A CIP catalogue record for this book is available from the British Library.

ISBN 0 00 218327 7 (paperback)
ISBN 0 00 218376 5 (hardback)

Commissioning Editor: Michael Doggart
Senior Editor: Lynne Gregory
Designer: Peter Laws
Illustrator: Simon Roulstone

This book was designed and produced by
Amanuensis Books Ltd
12 Station Road
Didcot
Oxfordshire
OX11 7LL

Printed in China

The pronoun 'he' has been used throughout and should be
interpreted as applying equally to men and women as appropriate.
It is important in sport, as elsewhere, that women and men should
have equal status and opportunities.

CONTENTS

THE AUTHOR

David Hewitt is a knowledgeable and experienced Senior Coach with the English Table Tennis Association based predominantly in North West England.

He has taught extensively, working with players of all ages and abilities, a number of whom have gone on to achieve both National and International success. More recently, he has devoted much of his time to helping several of England's leading disabled players.

In his collaboration with National Team Trainer Donald Parker and former European Womens Champion, Jill Parker (née Hammersley) he has co-written a series of books on the game. In this guide, he explains all you need to know to start teaching table tennis to a bunch of raw beginners who may have never picked up a bat in their lives!

INTRODUCTION

So you want to be a coach?

The main problem with the term 'coach' is that it embraces so much. If it's a label that's about to be hung on you, it should come as no great shock that you are expected to be all things to all men.

Look at the different hats you've got to wear for a start. You're an organizer, leader, motivator, assessor, spectator, manager, politician, psychiatrist, magician and, if you're good at your job, you might even become someone's idol! The list is endless. Then there are all the things you end up having to do; spending hours on the 'phone fixing up sessions and players, setting up the tables, running the session, putting the tables away, driving the bus to far-flung places, spending hours in draughty halls watching endless matches, providing a shoulder to cry on, ripping your hair out in exasperation, listening to hard luck stories, joining in celebrations, screaming, getting screamed at ...

If you happen to be a parent or a schoolteacher, it's likely that a lot of this will be familiar territory. For others it is not so it is worth reflecting a while, being honest with yourself about the true reasons for your involvement in the coaching of table tennis. There are good reasons and equally bad reasons, or put another way, there are individuals who make good coaches and there are others who do not. If you've come into coaching as a player who simply wants to help others to learn and enjoy the game, then you have nothing to fear. If you're an enthusiastic teacher who wants to see table tennis occupy a greater part of the school's PE curriculum, please join us. If you happen to be a parent who wants to know more to help youngsters improve, you are welcome.

If, on the other hand, you are a failed player who's looking for another means of getting into the limelight, or you are simply looking for a captive audience to perform in front of, perhaps you should think again. The rewards to be gained from teaching table tennis are rarely material. If you are ever lucky enough to get to a stage where you are paid to coach, be thankful if it covers your telephone bill. The real thrills don't always lie in working with the best and most talented players because, for them, success comes naturally. Working with beginners presents a different challenge altogether and in many respects, it is a more difficult one. It requires all the initiative, imagination and patience you can muster but there is a thrilling amount of satisfaction to be gained.

If you fail in your job and do not equip these people with the foundations of a solid technique and a good level of basic skill, then they may never go on to fulfil their true potential. It's interesting to note that both the Swedes and Chinese, two of the world's most successful table tennis nations, deploy their best coaches to the task of teaching beginners.

The characteristics of a good coach

Let's debunk one myth to start with: you don't have to be a good player to become a good coach. Many top players have strayed into coaching in the past but have failed miserably because of an inability to communicate well or because they are poor organizers.

Here are a few dos and don'ts to bear in mind now that you have made the decision to become a coach:

• Try at all times to gain and keep the respect of your players otherwise you will struggle to get your message across. This means looking the part and wearing appropriate clothes. First impressions are vital;

• Be organized and plan the content of each of your sessions thoroughly;

• Don't assume you are more important than the players. Your role is a supportive one which should not occupy the centre of the stage. This is the area reserved for the performer, not the director;

• Avoid the terms 'never' and 'always' when coaching table tennis technique. There have been too many examples in the past of world champions whose playing styles have been such that you might as well rewrite all the text books;

• Swap ideas with other coaches; there is nothing wrong with stealing and adapting from others in an effort to improve;

• Swap players with other coaches. It's impossible to be successful with every player that you work with. If you're not getting through to someone, don't be afraid to ask a colleague to have a go. Equally, don't hold someone back by keeping them in your group when they could benefit from playing amongst players of a higher standard;

• Get on the side of the parents - after all, they are the personal managers of the performers, providing the transport and financial backing if necessary. Listen to their worries and concerns and involve them in the child's development in the game;.

• Be realistic and don't expect too much from your players. Your aim is to get the individual to perform to the full extent of his potential, no matter how limited that might be. 'Do your best' is infinitely preferable to 'You must win this one';

• Lastly, keep it interesting. If it isn't fun to play then they won't come back next week and you will be out of a job.

David Hewitt

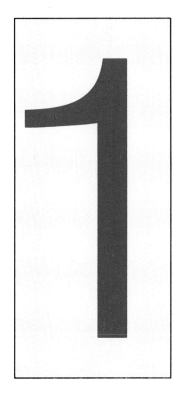

EQUIPMENT

Equipment

One of the boasts made by table tennis experts is that the game can be played virtually anywhere. Unlike a tennis court, a table tennis table is portable and adaptable and can be moved in a matter of minutes from one location to the next. In many ways, however, its profile as a dynamic sport has suffered because of this very adaptability. More often than not, if the best facilities are required by other sports, table tennis tables tend to be shifted into an adjacent anteroom hidden from view. This is always disappointing as not only is the game losing valuable opportunities to create an impact and attract newcomers, but also it rarely does the players any favours as lighting is likely to be poor, the floor uneven or the space restricted.

Therefore, the first consideration is to ensure that you have a suitable environment in which to play. Make sure that the lighting is adequate and visibility is even; that the floor gives good grip and lets the table sit evenly; that there is sufficient runback behind the tables and enough space between them to prevent the players from bumping into one another and injuring themselves.

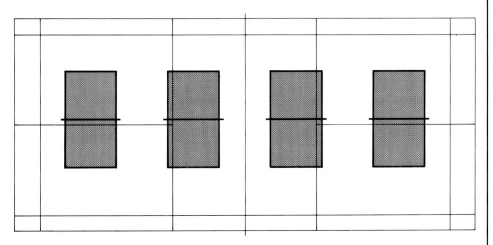

Tables

Table tennis tables are either foldaway or the standard static type, each of which have their advantages and disadvantages. The one you choose will very much depend on the situation in which the game is going to be played and the general standard of player who will be using it. The foldaway is easy to move as it sits as a complete unit on an undercarriage of wheels which detracts when the table is not in use. Furthermore, it takes only a matter of seconds to make ready for play. This type of table is ideal for beginners and with a little supervision can be erected by the youngest of players.

The static or standard table is a much more solid affair and once assembled gives a truer and more consistent bounce than the foldaway. For this reason, it tends to be preferred by more experienced players of league standard and above. Although it consists of two separate halves, the drawback is that the table is awkward and heavy to handle and move around.

Four tables can be accommodated quite easily on an area the size of one badminton court.

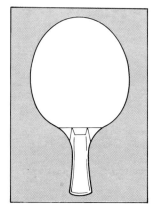

The shape of a modern table tennis bat

Choosing a Bat

The commercial success of sports equipment manufacturers and retailers in recent years has been to bestow table tennis bats with an aura of magic and mythology. The range now available is massive and is compounded by the trend to have a bat 'made to measure', with a choice of the blade and two rubber surfaces which cover it. There are a number of detailed and complex laws set down by the International Table Tennis Federation (ITTF), the governing body of the sport, which regulates the design of table tennis bats. Each side of the bat should be clearly different in colour and the rubber should be stamped with the ITTF logo of approval. Virtually all manufacturers comply with the required legal specification, so the danger of buying an 'illegal weapon' is now very remote.

As far as the beginner is concerned, the real danger lies in being tricked into spending a fortune and ending up with an expensive item which requires a high level of skill, touch and experience to use to full effect. Advise a beginner when selecting a bat to make sure that it is the 'all round' type. Careful inspection will usually reveal these very words stamped on the rubber. Ideally, it should be the reverse 'sandwich' type in which the pimples of the outer layer face inwards and are joined to the sponge layer. This sponge layer should preferably be no more than one and a half millimetres thick. If it is any thicker than this, the ability to control the ball will be made noticeably more difficult.

Bearing in mind that control is the most important factor for a beginner, it follows that similar attention should also be paid to the choice of blade. Firstly, make sure that the handle is comfortable so that it feels like a natural extension of the hand itself. Secondly, bearing in mind that the type of wood and number of ply affects the speed characteristic of the bat, a blade of five ply medium hardwood is ideal for beginners.

As a player becomes more experienced and proficient, the choice of bat becomes more significant but, nevertheless, the following ground rules still apply:

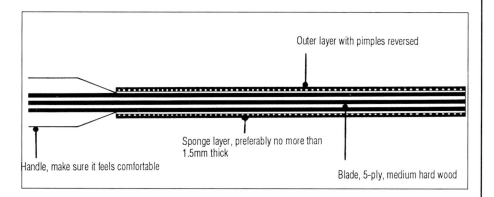

Outer layer with pimples reversed

Sponge layer, preferably no more than 1.5mm thick

Handle, make sure it feels comfortable

Blade, 5-ply, medium hard wood

• The thicker the wood, the faster the bat
• The thicker and harder the rubber, the faster the bat
• The greater the 'grip' characteristic of the rubber, the more spin can be imparted (pimpled out rubber imparts relatively little spin).

The various layers that make up a typical table tennis bat.

A bat of the 'all round' variety is relatively inexpensive and there is no reason why the blade cannot be re-covered at a later stage. All rubber ultimately loses its grip on the ball and becomes stale and smooth. Equally, once the player has acquired a sound level of control, a good technique and a degree of skill, he may need to add more pace and spin to the game and a more sophisticated type of rubber may become necessary.

There is always a danger, though, that too much attention can be focused on the various characteristics and properties of the bat and not enough on good technique. Table tennis players are notorious for blaming their misfortune on their bats but it is always the bad workman who blames his tools.

Balls

There are two types of table tennis ball, plastic and celluloid. Although the plastic ones are the most durable, they are less common nowadays and, indeed, less popular among experienced players. The quality of the ball is determined by the star rating conferred on it by the ITTF, with three stars representing the best and most consistent on the market. The one- and two-star balls may be suitable for practice purposes, but are rarely used in any formally organized competition.

Clothing and Footwear

It's all too tempting with a sport such as ours to say that all you need are gym shoes and a bat. Clearly, we do not want to turn away anyone who wants to join in and discover the game, but at the same time, we should also be wary of conveying a sloppy image. This is, after all, a sport in the truest sense and when played at a high level, is physically demanding and very athletic.

Even with a group of beginners, there is a lot to be said for encouraging a basic uniform of white gym shoes, white socks, dark shorts and T-shirt. None of these items should break the bank. Discourage the wearing of white or light-coloured shorts and shirts as light-coloured clothing runs the risk of being deemed contrary to the laws governing clothing.

Because sport shoes have become a fashion accessory among many youngsters, it shouldn't be too difficult to enforce this part of the outfit. Most lightweight training shoes will be suitable as long as they give good adhesion to the floor and, if possible, support around the instep part of the foot.

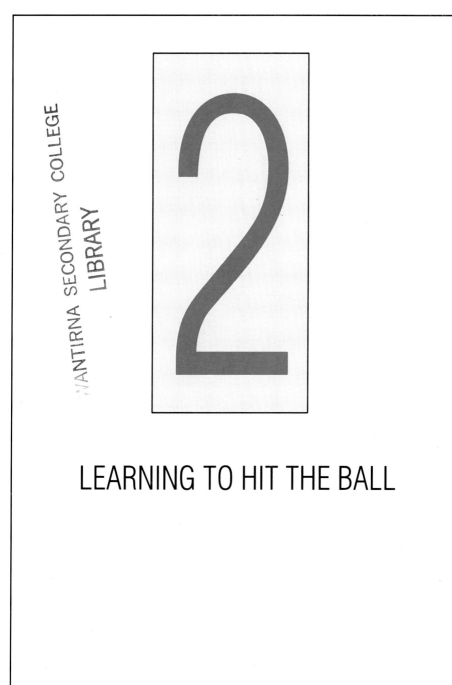

LEARNING TO HIT THE BALL

Learning to Hit the Ball

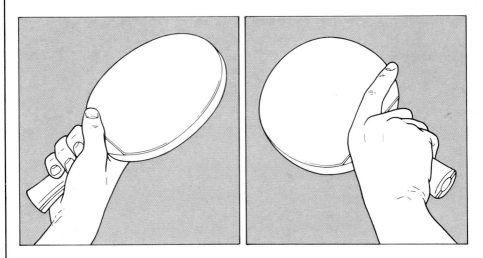

The **shakehand grip** as seen from the forehand side (left) and the backhand side (right).

For a player to derive any enjoyment, feeling of participation, satisfaction or ultimate success from a ball game, be it cricket, tennis, badminton or table tennis, it is vital to be able to hit a moving ball. For many people, this is a simple and intuitive act requiring no guidance or support at all. For others without a natural sense of coordination, it can be a nightmare.

Before looking at ways in which hand-to-eye coordination can be nurtured and improved, the way in which the bat is held needs to be considered.

The Grip

In a sense, there is only one way to hold a table tennis bat and that is with the grip that feels most comfortable for the player. Unfortunately, this simple rule does not always produce a grip which is suited to playing the game well. With the chosen grip it should be possible to make an instantaneous, fine adjustment to the angle of the bat to control the direction of the ball. There

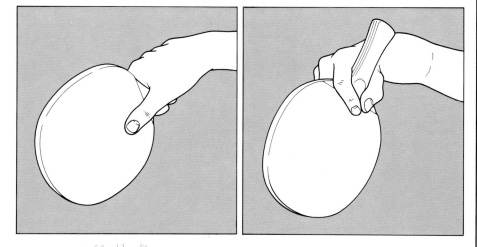

should be no need to alter the grip between the forehand and backhand sides during a rally as table tennis is too fast a game to allow for this sort of luxury. As a result there are two established grips, the 'shakehold', preferred by most European and Western players and the 'penhold' adopted by many Asian players.

The 'shakehold' grip is achieved by literally shaking hands with the handle of the bat. The forefinger should be placed on the bottom part of the backhand side of the blade, and the thumb should rest on the centre part of the forehand side near to the neck of the handle. The remaining three fingers wrap firmly, but not too tightly, around the handle. A useful tip for judging whether the grip is too tight is to check the whiteness of the knuckles. If they are white then the player clearly needs to relax the grip or control of movement will be inhibited. This type of grip may initially feel awkward to the beginner who may well want to adjust it in some way. It's important, though, to keep correcting a bad grip because it can lead to untold difficulties at a later stage.

'Penhold' is also a very apt description for the second of the two most popular grips in the game. Here the thumb and forefinger

Top left: Watch out for this typical beginner's fault with the shakehand grip; with the thumb pressing on the blade like this, forehand shots become very awkward.
Top right: The **penhold grip**, favoured by millions of Asian players.

close around the neck of the bat handle at the point where it meets the blade, in much the same way in which you might hold a pen. The remaining fingers can either be splayed across the other side of the blade or alternatively cupped. The distinguishing feature of the penhold grip is that only one side of the bat is used throughout to hit the ball.

Because of this, bats designed exclusively for players using the penhold grip are available with rubber covering one side of the bat and an ergonomic handle.

On balance the shakehold grip is probably the easier of the two grips to master as it gives the most flexibility. Nevertheless, it's worth bearing in mind that there are millions of Chinese youngsters learning with the penhold type of grip every day, and it is China which has been a dominating force in the game since the early 1960s.

Although both grips appear very different from one another, they both have one important thing in common. The thumb and the forefinger are positioned in such a way as to enable delicate and instant control to be exercised over the angle of the bat throughout play.

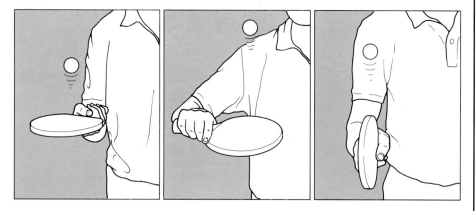

Coordination

There are a couple of quick and simple tests which a coach can use to gauge whether a player is coordinated, and these can be performed without having to pick up a bat or ball. Rubbing the stomach with one hand and patting the head with the other at the same time is one useful exercise; swinging the arms in big circles from the shoulders with one arm going in one direction and the other arm in the opposite direction is another. The proficiency with which these tasks are performed can be a good indication of the likely level of coordination. However, do not write off an individual who appears at first sight to be awkward and clumsy as this does not always mean he will not make a useful player.

Hand-to-eye coordination, touch and early ball skills can be developed by one or two simple off-the-table exercises. The most obvious of these is bouncing the ball on the bat, which is also a useful opportunity to introduce and establish the correct grip. This exercise can be slowly developed in a progressive way to enhance the control of the would-be player over the moving ball. The next stage would be to:
• Bounce the ball at a consistent height
• Bounce the ball at a consistent height on the backhand of the bat
• Alternate bounces between the two sides

Practise bouncing the ball using only the forehand side of the bat (far left), the backhand side of the bat (centre) and the edge of the bat (above) which requires an even higher level of coordination and concentration.

• Introduce the bouncing of the ball on the blade edge of the bat into any of these exercises.

As well as the ability to coordinate the hand and react to the continually varying movement of the ball, judging where and when to make contact, the player also needs to gain control over the force with which it is struck. A simple and effective way of isolating this particular aspect of ball control is to practise volleying the ball repeatedly against a wall. Unlike a squash ball which is comparatively soft and lacks a high degree of bounce, table tennis balls are quite the opposite. In this exercise you will discover that it does not require much force for the ball to rebound too fast for the average beginner to make a successful second or third shot.

From the coach's point of view, a valuable piece of information emerges from these simple exercises. Ball control is easier when the bat, and therefore the ball, is kept close to the head and upper body. Conversely it becomes progressively more difficult to perform as the playing arm becomes extended and the bat is held further away. This is a useful factor to bear in mind when the first attempts at play on the table take place.

WHAT'S IN A SHOT?

What's in a Shot ?

Before we look at the four strokes which form the basis of the game as it exists today, it's worth considering the principles involved in strokeplay: in other words, the key elements in producing a shot which constitute good technique. In table tennis this is usually broken down into seven separate areas, which are common to virtually every shot in the game. They are:

1. Stance
2. Table position
3. Length
4. Timing
5. Body action
6. Bat arm and bat angle
7. Free arm.

To identify faults or weaknesses in technique, it is essential that a coach fully appreciates the part played by each of these factors. Together they form the 'magnificent seven' - an invaluable checklist which can be used as a comprehensive way of analyzing a player's technique.

Stance

Considering that an incorrect stance is at the root of many players' problems, it's surprising how little attention is paid by coaches to this crucial feature.

Table tennis is a fast one-to-one game with little time for recovery between shots. It makes sense then that the stance adopted should allow the player to move efficiently, at speed, to various parts of the table and at the same time maintain good balance, steady vision and control over the stroke.

The optimum stance for table tennis is shown in the diagram opposite. Working from the feet upwards, the significant points to bear in mind are that:

• The feet are spread as wide apart as the shoulders.

The right stance

• The knees are bent slightly and projected inwards a little so that the weight of the body shifts to the balls of the feet at the front instep. This enables the player to spring quickly from side to side.
• The upper body is arched forward so that there is space between the bat arm and the lower chest to enable arm movement to be unrestricted. A good tip is to check that the chin is about in line vertically with the knees.

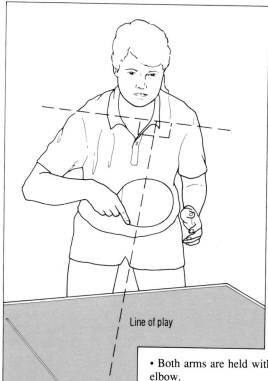

Line of play

Always aim for the shoulders to be square to the line of play. This would be the position of the upper body for a backhand push played across the diagonal.

• Both arms are held with an angle of about 90 degrees at the elbow.
• The player's position when playing the ball, which changes throughout the duration of the rally, should always be what is termed 'relative to the line of play'. With the exception, possibly of one or two of the more advanced defensive shots, this is invariably **square to the line of play**. A simple way to illustrate this is to point out that after the shot is played, the player's shoulders and chest should end up facing the direction in which the ball is hit. The feet will also be pointing in the same direction, roughly in line with the shoulders.

A final word on stance. It's impossible to be definitive about the precise angle of the bend of the knees or to what degree the upper body should be crouched forward or the exact width to which the feet should be apart. All these factors will be affected by the height of the individual in question. It will be of little help to the youngster who can barely peer over the table to insist that he keeps his feet as wide apart as his shoulders. This will only make his stance problem worse, so a coach should use his intelligence, be flexible and make allowances for the individual. If you are dealing with a seven-foot giant, instruct him to widen his base beyond the width of the shoulders so that he can focus better on the ball.

Position of player in relation to table

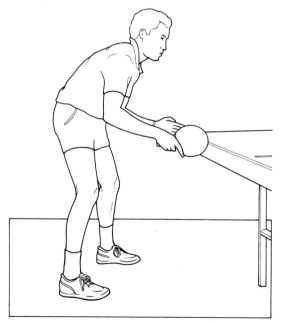

Table Position

It helps youngsters learning the game to maintain a position which is relatively close to the table. Not only does it help give them a good timing point but it is also a bit easier to hit accurately into the target area which, for most newcomers, will simply be the other side of the net. The further away from the table, the harder this becomes. The ideal distance is probably the point, once the correct stance has been adopted, where the bat is barely touching the edge of the table.

Length

In the initial stages of learning the game, the swing of the playing arm should be kept short. A long swing makes it harder to keep control over the speed and direction of the ball. The length and swing of any shot can be broken down into three distinct phases: the time when the bat is accelerating in the swing, the point at which contact is made with the ball and, lastly, the follow-through when the bat arm is slowing down.

Not only is a short swing necessary, but it is important to bear in mind that the main part of the stroke - probably 70 per cent of the energy exerted - should be devoted to the acceleration phase. A player hitting the ball too early in the swing will have difficulty later in learning to generate power to hit the ball hard.

Timing

Some players, picking up a bat for the first time, will instinctively want to hit the ball late in its bounce. They find it hard to do otherwise, because they feel they need time to react and think about the shot before striking the ball. You often find that this type of individual makes a good defensive player in which the bulk of their game is played some distance away from the table.

However, unless the player feels totally uncomfortable, you should try and teach 'peak of the bounce' timing. The main

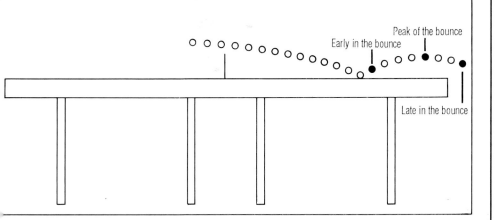

benefit to be gained from hitting the ball at the highest point of the bounce is that at this point the greatest part of the target area, that is, the other side of the net, becomes available. As the ball drops away from its peak, it becomes more difficult to hit down on to the other side. What inevitably happens is that the player tries to compensate by hitting underneath the ball and lobbing it up in the hope that it lands somewhere on the other side. Alternatively, there is a tendency to curve and brush the ball, to try and make it loop up and dip down over the net.

In table tennis, we talk of three timing points - early in the bounce, peak or top of the bounce and late in the bounce.

Body Action

It's a popular misconception that the only part of the body that gains any exercise value from table tennis is the playing arm. This is nonsense! Any top player will tell you that the whole of the body is utilized in a match. Even with the basic strokes in the game, you will soon appreciate the contribution that the legs, waist and shoulders make in developing, for example, a hard, aggressive forehand drive.

Bat Arm and Bat Angle

We have already touched on the way in which ball control is affected as the bat arm becomes more extended. It is important when you come to introduce a new stroke that you are aware, for example, of the best angle at which the elbow should be held for maximum effect.

You should consider the bat arm in much the same way as you might regard a whip. Each of its three joints contributes in a different way. The shoulder is like the handle of a whip and although it doesn't move fast, it is the source of the power which will ultimately be transmitted to the bat. The elbow moves slightly faster but lacks the strength and power of the shoulder. The wrist is the head of the whip and the fastest moving part of the arm but, equally, it is the weakest. All three joints need to be fluid, synchronized and working in such a way that they complement each other.

A further factor which will have a critical influence on whether the ball clears the net and lands on the other side of the table, is the angle at which the bat is held. This can either be 'open' or 'closed' as illustrated opposite.

Free Arm

This is the last of the seven points on our checklist. Proper use of the free arm helps the rotation of the body, particularly in the power shots. Its greatest contribution as far as the beginner is concerned, however, is in helping to coordinate the process of stroke production and connecting bat with ball. By using the free arm as a sort of gun sight to point at the ball, it can often make all the difference between hitting and missing.

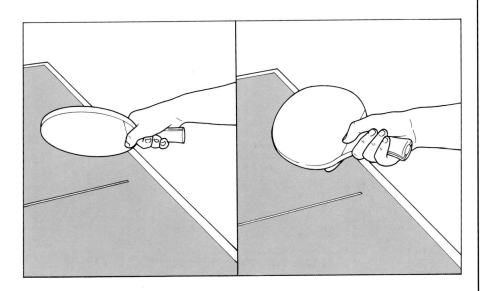

Left: A closed bat angle
Right: An open bat angle

Summary

The seven key technical points which need to be taken into account in introducing any new stroke and developing the skills involved are:
• Stance
• Table position
• Length
• Timing
• Body action
• Bat arm and bat angle
• Free arm.

From the coach's point of view, they can be used as an analytical checklist and a basis from which to identify faults and correct and improve poor technique. Be careful not to bombard your pupils with too much information at once. Each of the points considered needs to be covered gradually. Therefore, when introducing a new stroke, concentrate initially on getting the stance, timing point, bat arm and bat angle right. Deal with the remaining four points successively; how long this takes will very much depend on your patience and the receptiveness of your players.

BUILDING THE BASIC GAME

Building the Basic Game

There are essentially four basic strokes in table tennis, which together form the cornerstone of today's modern game. They are:
• The 'backhand push' from which the backhand backspin or the defensive chop strokes stem.
• The 'forehand' drive which forms the basis of the forehand smash, block, fast drive and topspin shots.
• The 'backhand drive' which can also be developed into a topspin stroke or blocking stroke.
• The 'forehand push' which can also be easily varied to become a backspin or chopping stroke.

This chapter examines each of these fundamental strokes and looks at the typical pitfalls encountered by beginners in the learning process. It also suggests one or two practices which can be coached to correct a fault, together with some useful exercises and games, designed both to groove in the shot and, at the same time, provide some enjoyment for those taking part. All the strokes are described as if they are being performed by a right-handed player. For left-handers, the same principles apply but read 'right' for 'left' and vice versa.

Backhand Push

This is probably the easiest of all the four basic shots to learn. It's a gentle shot and is often used early on in a rally to keep the ball short and low to prevent the opponent from attacking. There is hardly any body movement involved and the stoke is produced at the elbow, with the bat held in a slightly open angle and travelling in a downwards direction to strike the back of the ball at the peak of the bounce. The feet and shoulders should all be square and facing the area of the table to where the ball is to be played. Whenever possible, the ball should be played just to the left of the stomach and not outside the body. This will make it easier to keep control over the direction of the ball. It follows then, that the player positions his body to where the ball is about to bounce, before the stroke is played. The correct stance, therefore, is all important.

Looking at the stroke in terms of the seven point checklist, it breaks down like this:
Length: Short
Timing: Peak
Table position: Close
Stance: Square
Body action: Nil
Free arm: Points to the ball
Bat arm and bat angle: Produced from the elbow, with the bat slightly open.

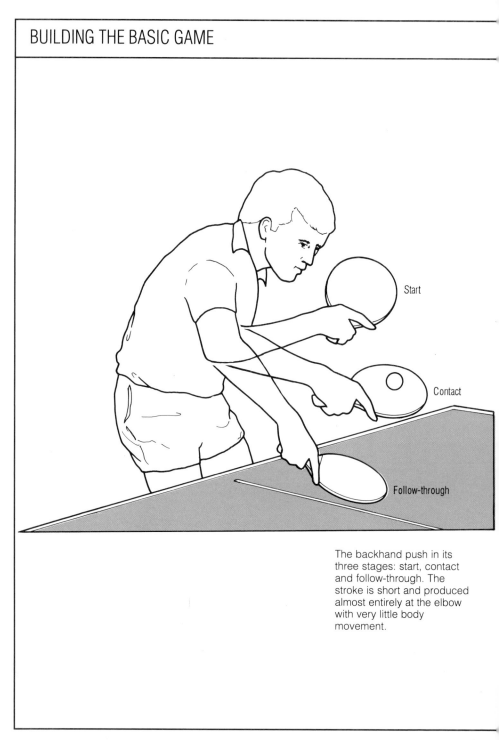

Start

Contact

Follow-through

The backhand push in its three stages: start, contact and follow-through. The stroke is short and produced almost entirely at the elbow with very little body movement.

Fault correction

Problem: The player is hitting the ball too high.
Remedy: Check the bat angle to see whether by being too open the bat is making contact withs the underneath of the ball and forcing it upwards. Check that the shot is being played using only the elbow, as many beginners tend to use the shoulder and lock the elbow joint. This can also have the effect of forcing the ball upwards.

Problem: The player has difficulty in playing the ball to a consistent length and overhits the end of the table.
Remedy: Check the grip. If the bat is being held too tight the arm will be stiff and it will be impossible for the player to develop touch and feel the ball making contact with the bat. Check the length of the stroke as well, as too much variation in swing will affect the distance the ball travels.

A backhand push correctly performed, below right, as compared with one incorrectly performed, below left. Note how in the incorrect illustration the free arm is trailing, the bat angle is incorrect, the grip is poor and the right leg leading instead of the left.

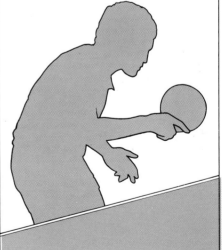

Introduce the backhand push by getting the players to play along the shortest diagonal, as shown by the bats numbered 1 in the diagram. As they become more proficient, bring the players further apart, in stages, as shown by the sets of bats numbered 2 and 3.

The main thing to remember about the backhand push is that it is a stroke used to control and contain play. Practices should be designed with this in mind with particular emphasis on consistency in both height and length. Whenever possible, try to avoid setting up practice routines where the shot is being played from the player's forehand side of the table as this is an unnatural occurrence in match play. With four right handed players on the table, however, it becomes unavoidable and in this situation vary the practice by playing 'down the line' as well as across the diagonal.

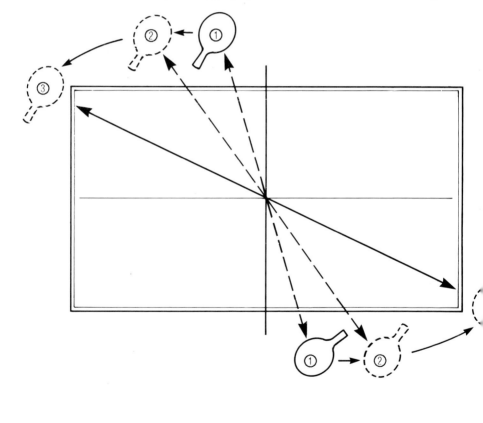

Exercises

For developing short 'touch' control the practice shown opposite is useful. It is especially valuable in helping those players who have difficulty in playing the ball to a consistent length. As a consistent stroke emerges, bring the players further back from the net in gradual stages.

Because there are not too many practise permutations possible with the backhand push, you might wish to try the following two fun games as a way of sustaining interest.

Game 1. This is a good way of occupying four or more players on one table in an energetic way. Player 1 plays a backhand push along the diagonal shown to Player 2 who returns it also with a backhand push to Player 3 and so on, with all the players circulating around the table. Penalties can be introduced, for example, the first player to make a mistake has to perform five sit-ups or press-ups.

A useful spin off of this game is that it stimulates mobility.

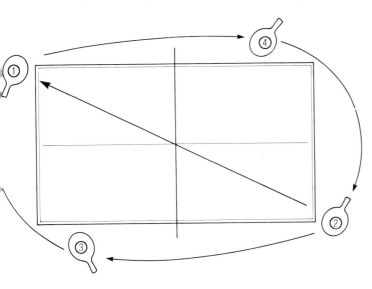

Game 2

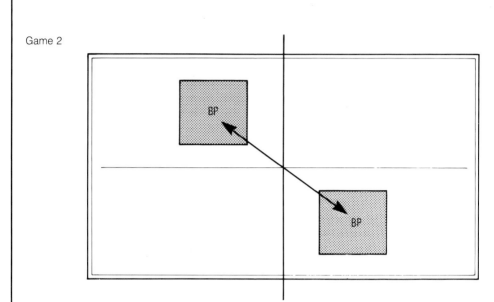

Game 2. Using only the backhand push, both players must keep the ball within the area of two sheets of A4 paper joined together, which is chalked on the table. Play games of eleven up with points awarded when mistakes occur, including those occasions when the ball fails to hit the target area.

A target-related exercise such as this need not be restricted to the backhand push. It is designed to improve accuracy and also introduces a competitive element into a coaching session.

Forehand Drive

Unlike the backhand stroke, virtually all forehand shots are generated from a side to square stance. In the case of a right-handed player, this means that the left foot should be leading the right slightly. The shot is produced from the shoulder with the elbow held at an angle of about 90° and the bat slightly closed. The bat moves forwards and in an upwards direction to strike the back of the ball at the peak of its bounce. At the same time, the weight should shift from the right to the left leg and the upper body should rotate so that the shoulders end up square to the line of play.

The follow-through finishes at a point roughly in line with the nose. Throughout the stroke, make sure that the free arm is running parallel with the playing arm and is being used to track the ball. It also plays an important part in helping the body to rotate in the manner described.

In terms of our seven point checklist, the forehand drive has the following characteristics:

Length: Medium
Timing: Peak
Table position: Close
Stance: Side to square
Body action: Rotating slightly
Free arm: Points to the ball and helps balance and rotation of the body
Bat arm and bat angle: Produced from the shoulder and parallel to the free arm with the bat slightly closed.

The forehand drive, in its three stages: start, contact and follow-through. Note how the approach to the stroke is with a side to square stance but with the shoulders finishing, nonetheless, square to the line of play.

Fault correction

Problem: The player keeps overhitting
Remedy: Check that the bat angle is being kept sufficiently closed to ensure that the ball will be moving in a downward trajectory. Also, make sure that contact is being made on, or even slightly before, the peak of the bounce and not too late.

Problem: The player is unable to control the direction of the ball.
Remedy: Check the stance and body action. Are the feet side to square or is the body too sideways on? Are the shoulders finishing facing where the ball is to be played?

To encourage consistency, issue a challenge to the group and ask for the first table to produce ten, then 15, 20 and so on, good continuous strokes. The players on the losing tables have to perform five sit-ups, burpees or star jumps. If there's a wide disparity of ability in the group, handicap the more able pairs by imposing a higher target than the rest.

A forehand drive correctly performed (below right) as compared to one incorrectly performed (below left). Note how in the incorrect shot illustration, the stance is too sideways on and leaning back, the free arm is trailing, the grip is too cocked up and the body is cramping the playing arm.

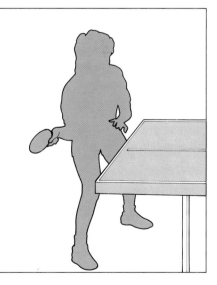

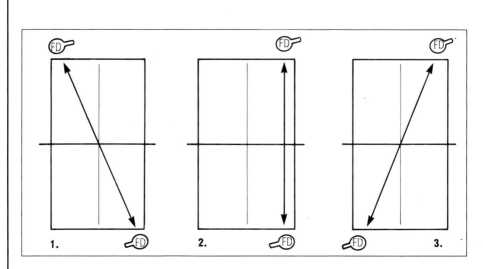

BD - Backhand drive
FD - Forehand drive
BD/FD - Alternative
backhand drive and forehand
drive

Exercise 1 is a
straightforward forehand to
forehand drive (FD) using the
diagonal - the longest part
of the table. Exercise 2 is the
same routine but played
down the line. Exercise 3 is
played using the backhand
diagonal. In all cases make
sure that the stroke is
performed with the upper
body facing square to the
line of play and that the ball
is kept moving at a steady
pace and not too fast.

Backhand Drive

This stroke is played with the feet in the same position as the backhand push, in line with the shoulders and facing the area of the table to where the ball is to be played. With the bat held at a slightly closed angle, the stroke starts just to the left of the body. Using the elbow, which should be held at about 90° or so, the bat moves forward in an upward direction, striking the back of the ball at the peak of the bounce, at a point which is just about left of centre of the stomach. At the point of contact, the wrist should be turning and folding the bat over the ball so that the stroke finishes with the forehand side of the blade visible to the player. The points to look for in a good backhand drive are:

Length: Medium
Timing: Peak
Table position: Close
Stance: Square
Body action: Nil
Free arm: Points to the ball
Bat arm and bat angle: Produced from the elbow and wrist with a closed bat.

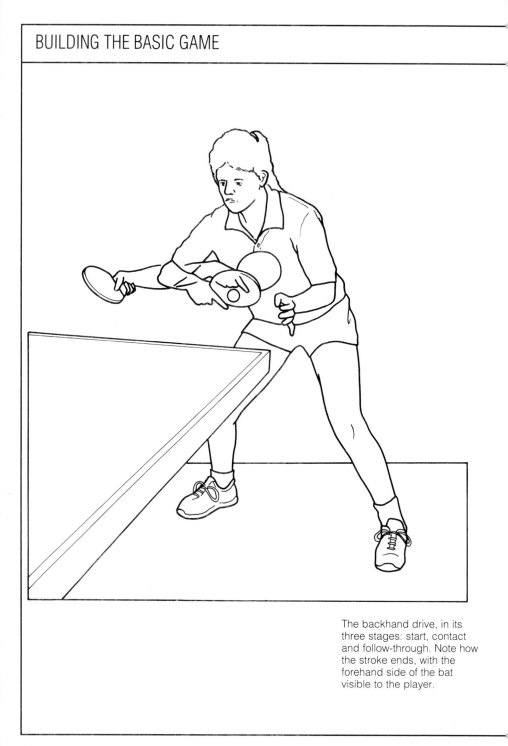

The backhand drive, in its three stages: start, contact and follow-through. Note how the stroke ends, with the forehand side of the bat visible to the player.

Fault Correction

Problem: The player is failing to turn the wrist and close the angle of the bat.

Remedy: Try placing a stationary ball on an open bat and tell the player to toss the ball like a sling shot over to the other side of the table. Without turning the wrist and folding the bat over thereby closing the angle of the bat, this will prove impossible.

Problem: The player is stretching for the ball when it is played wide or when it is played tight into the body, cramping the shot.

Remedy: The short answer to both of these difficulties is 'move your feet!' Make sure that the player positions himself to where the ball is played so that contact is made under the chin and in front of the stomach.

Apart from playing across the backhand diagonal, there is a limit to what you can do with this shot. Now is the time to combine this shot with the forehand drive.

A backhand drive correctly performed (below right) as compared to one incorrectly performed (below left). Note how in the incorrect shot illustration: the free arm is trailing; the thumb is pushing against the blade of the bat; the stroke is being produced from outside the line of the body instead of slightly to the left of the stomach; the right foot is leading the left which inhibits movement to the player's right for forehand shots.

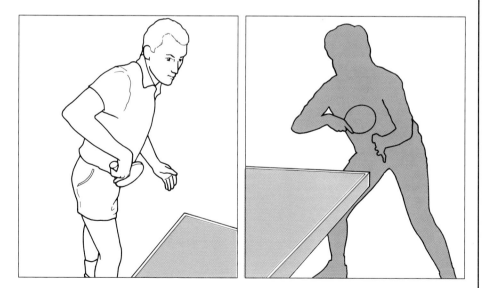

45

BUILDING THE BASIC GAME

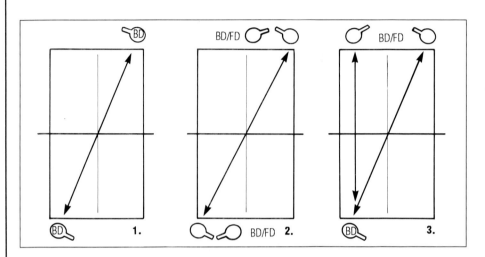

In Exercises 2 and 3, it is important that the players move their feet as economically as possible in order to maintain a stance which leaves them square to the line of play.

Forehand Push

Beginners tend to find this stroke the toughest of the lot. Its use and purpose in matchplay is the same as the backhand push and it requires a good deal of practise to master properly. The stance is the same as in the forehand drive - slightly side to square - but as with all strokes, the shoulders and upper body should finish the stroke square to the line of play. The shot is produced from the elbow and requires very little swing but it should not be a jerky action or the ball will fly off the bat. Held in an open angle, the bat moves forwards in a slightly downwards direction, hitting the back of the ball at the peak of the bounce and finishing just above the surface of the table. Although not quite as pronounced as the forehand drive, there should still be a little body rotation and the free arm, as always, can be used to pick out the ball and help with the balance.

To help control, encourage the player to get his head as close as possible to the ball without actually impeding the stroke. Using the checklist once more, the forehand push breaks down as follows:

Length: Short
Timing: Peak
Table position: Close
Stance: Slightly side to square
Body action: Rotating slightly
Free arm: Points to the ball and helps balance
Bat arm and bat angle: Produced from the elbow with slightly open blade.

The forehand push in its three stages: start, contact and follow-through. This short stroke often represents, for many beginners, the most difficult of the four basic strokes.

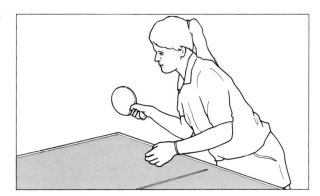

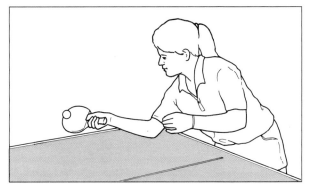

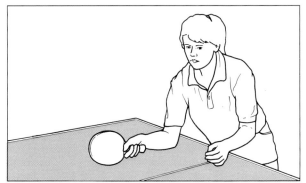

Fault Correction

Problem: The player has a tendency to alter the angle of the bat during the stroke and the shot starts to develop into a distorted version of the forehand drive.

Remedy: Insist that the leading edge of the bat, that is the bottom part, lightly touches the table at the end of the follow-through. This will make sure that the bat is moving downwards and not across or upwards.

Instead of playing across the diagonal, set up the practice so that the stroke is played to a variety of positions on the table. Both players will have to take care that their stances are appropriately adjusted to maintain a continuous rally.

A forehand push correctly performed (below right) as compared to one incorrectly performed (below left). Note how in the incorrect shot the player is too far away from the ball, the bat angle is too closed and therefore good control will be difficult to maintain.

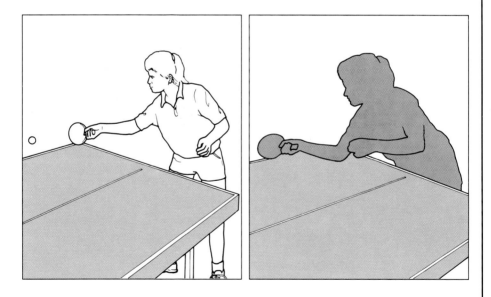

49

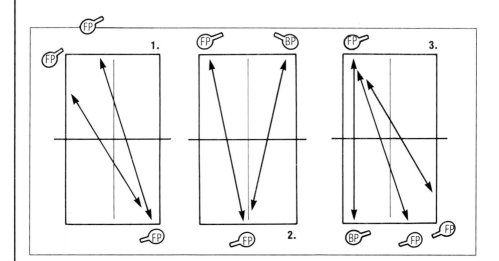

The push is a much softer, more delicate stroke and it is important to maintain good control throughout, particularly on the forehand side. Ensure that the head is kept near to both bat and ball and that the player avoids the temptation to stretch when it is played wide, as in Exercise 3.

Summary

All the basic strokes are intended to be played with the ball taken at the peak of the bounce; this is very important. The timing point that players learn when they first start to play has a tendency to stick with them throughout their playing careers. If the ball is taken too late, then the player starts to make unconscious adjustments and may quite unnecessarily adopt a defensive style. Not that this is always a bad thing, but he may be an individual with talent who might otherwise have made a great attacker.

Both the Swedes and the Chinese pay great attention to this point in deciding which stroke to teach the beginner first. You don't always have to start with the backhand push, although this is probably the easiest of the four to pick up as far as beginners are concerned. However, there is nothing to stop you introducing the forehand drive first as the Swedes do. To play an effective forehand drive, the ball has to be taken at the peak of its bounce or even before. This is a good way of ensuring that newcomers get off to the right start as far as timing is concerned. There's also a school of thought which suggests that, at a much later stage in the playing career, youngsters taught in this way will not be afraid to attack their way out of difficulty when under pressure, instead of reverting to more negative pushing shots.

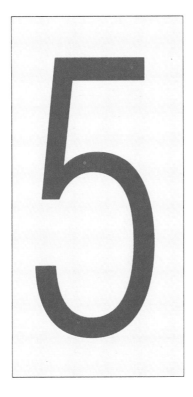

MOVEMENT, FOOTWORK
AND REACTION

Movement, Footwork and Reaction

Table tennis is a fast game played over a small area. It's easy for beginners to fall into the trap of stretching and reaching for the ball instead of moving the feet and body. But, like all bad habits, it becomes a hard one to kick at a later stage. It doesn't matter what stroke we are talking about, they are all that much easier to perform if the body is in the right position in relation to the ball.

So what are the main factors that affect a player's ability to move efficiently? No doubt there are plenty of scientific explanations which answer the question. The short answer though is that there are three as far as table tennis is concerned:

1. Footwork
2. Stability and balance
3. Weight transference.

We will look at the various types of **footwork** used in the game at a later stage in this chapter. Suffice it to say that there are two different patterns of footwork, each of which is used in its own way to respond to the typical situations that most players find themselves in during a game.

The Correct Stance

- A stance where the base is too narrow and the body is upright usually impedes the player's ability to keep good balance.
- A stance which is too wide and squat is very stable, but quick movement after a shot has been played is made very difficult.

Stability also affects movement. We have already looked at the important features of a good stance in Chapter 3. The need to make allowances for the physical characteristics of the player has also been mentioned. To recap, the ground rules to bear in mind with the stances are:

• A stance where the base is too narrow and the body is upright usually impedes the player's ability to keep good balance.
• A stance which is too wide and squat is very stable, but quick movement after a shot has been played is made very difficult.

Somewhere between the two lies the best stance for your player and it is usually the point where the centre of gravity is just above the base of the spine.

Weight transference is a technical expression which recognizes that there are several shots which require the player to transfer the body's weight from one foot to the other. This is particularly true of the forehand drive and all its related strokes. It is also especially important in the process of generating power and speed. The player has to be capable of transferring his body weight when moving to one side of the table or the other between strokes.

In terms of the player's development, the fundamentals of good economical footwork should be taught as soon as possible, preferably at the same time as the four basic strokes.

There are essentially two types of **footwork** used in the modern game, 'stepping footwork' and 'running footwork'. For the beginner, the former is the most appropriate. Stepping footwork is used close to the table and its main feature is that the feet do not cross one another. It's virtually a sideways, skipping movement which allows the player to maintain a solid stance and makes recovery easy once the shot is played. If the feet should cross when close up to the table, it's hard for players to recover stability especially if forced to move across to the other side of the table for the next ball.

Running footwork, on the other hand, is used further away from the table over a larger area. As its name suggests, it involves the feet and legs crossing each other in a normal running fashion. Because the player is away from the table, there is a little more time to effect recovery for the next ball.

Regular footwork

The main challenge facing a coach when trying to instil correct, but nimble, footwork in a player is to reach a stage where a footwork pattern becomes almost automatic. The player no longer has to think how and where to move the feet because it has become an instinctive process. We do this by using what is known as 'regular footwork exercises'. These are practices at the table, where the player knows in advance where the ball is going to be placed, for example, a series of forehand drives played alternately from the backhand and forehand wings of the table. Depending on natural talent and ability, the player eventually reaches a stage where the one or two steps involved become an almost unconscious process which should be repeated automatically in a game situation. Here are a few regular footwork exercises you might try in your practice sessions.

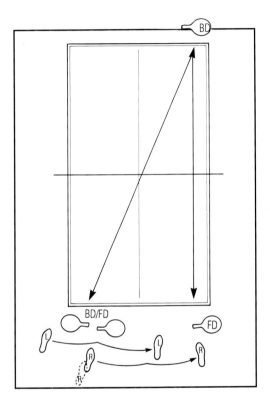

The footprints shown to the left of the table indicate the position of the feet for a backhand drive (BD) along the diagonal. For a forehand drive (FD) along the same diagonal, the right foot needs to be trailing the left slightly as shown by the dotted footprint. The footprints indicate the approximate position of the feet for a forehand drive down the line.

Exercise 1
Alternate forehand and backhand drives to a backhand block

This is played using the same diagonal. The main point to watch out for is that the player is shifting between a square (backhand) and side to square (forehand) stance. This exercise can be varied so that the forehand is played from the forehand wing to introduce a sideways, skipping movement as well. Make sure, though, that the weight is on the back foot and is being transferred through to the front when the forehand is being played.

55

Exercise 2

Irrespective of whether the ball is being played along the diagonal or down the line, the feet need to be positioned in such a way as to leave the upper body facing square to the line of play.

Exercise 2
Alternate forehand and backhand drives to a forehand block

This is very similar to Exercise 1 but the backhand needs to be played from a very square position to ensure that the ball is returned to the opponent's forehand wing. It can also be varied in the same way as Exercise 1 where the forehand is played diagonally across the table.

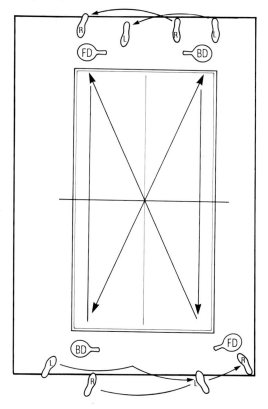

Irregular footwork exercises

A quick indication of whether a footwork pattern has been grooved into a player's subconscious is to test its effectiveness with an 'irregular' footwork exercise. This is an exercise which involves a switch in the direction of the ball at a point in the rally unknown to the player. It closely resembles a matchplay situation where the pace and direction of the ball will vary constantly during the rally. For example, using the backhand diagonal, the player hits a forehand drive to the opponent's backhand block. However, the opponent may switch any one of these balls down the forehand wing at any time.

All the regular footwork exercises described earlier can quite easily be adjusted slightly so that they become irregular. Irregular footwork exercises can be enhanced one stage further so that once the direction of the ball has been switched, both players then have the freedom to play the point out much as they might do in a match.

You may well find that the transition from regular to irregular practices is not without its snags. Some players can demonstrate beautiful footwork patterns if the practice involves the use of regular footwork. But when it comes to the more unpredictable irregular exercises, they seem to be either yards too late, or they tie themselves in knots. Why is this? Why do some individuals react with so much greater ease than others?

Exercise 3

Exercise 3
A combination exercise with both players hitting alternate forehand and backhand drives.

One player will always be playing across the table with the other playing down the line. This is a more advanced regular footwork exercise but should not be beyond the capability of most novices. But, as with any practice routine, if the players are spending most of their time picking the ball off the floor, then the exercise is too difficult. Go back to something easier and more manageable.

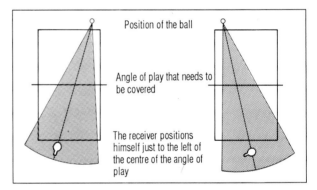

Position of the ball

Angle of play that needs to be covered

The receiver positions himself just to the left of the centre of the angle of play

The Three Rs - Reading, Reacting and Recovering

We are all born with different levels of natural ability and we all differ in the speed with which we are able to react to situations. The reason why some players seem to be in the right position almost before the ball has been struck is that their natural sense of anticipation is razor sharp. Although good anticipation is a gift you are born with, it can be improved upon simply by reading the other player's game and recovering to the best position in time for the next ball.

How often do you hear that immortal line 'Watch the ball!'? It's true, watching the ball is important but as far as table tennis is concerned, this expression should really be 'Watch the player!' By watching the opponent's body action and, in particular the opponent's bat, it is possible to pick up clues and read where the ball is likely to be hit. If a player is 'ball watching' and not 'player watching' it's likely that the necessary reaction is only going to occur when the ball is perhaps halfway across the net on its journey back. By watching the opponent's bat immediately before the ball is played, some slight advantage can be gained and his return shot can be understood a split second earlier. In the final analysis, this can mean the difference between always being on the defensive or instead being in a position to seize the initiative.

A good recovery position after the ball is played is another factor which can also aid anticipation. The position that a player recovers to after he has hit the ball is dictated entirely by the area on the table to which he has played the ball, and therefore, by the angle of play that is then made available to the opponent. In general, it should be just to the left of the centre of the angle available.

Some players do this without thinking, others have to be taught the principles involved and need to develop an awareness of angles of play (see Exercise 3). A useful way of demonstrating this is to recreate the angles by using two lengths of rope or washing-line to correspond with the boundaries of the angle of play shown which converge at the point from which the ball is to be struck. You will need three helpers from your group of players, one to hold the two ropes at one side of the table and two others to hold an end each at the opposite side. Start by asking the group to establish the angle of play available and then ask them where, in between the two ropes, is the point at which they think the receiving player should be positioned. You can also use this model as a vivid illustration of how the angle of play to be covered becomes wider the further away the striking player is positioned from the table.

Like good footwork, an awareness of angles of play and the need to anticipate are all good habits for the player to get into. None are what might be termed advanced techniques so there's no harm done by introducing them as soon as there is a good grasp of the four basic strokes.

SERVICE AND RECEIVE

Service and Receive

An outsider watching a game of local league table tennis could be forgiven for thinking that the service is simply a means of putting the ball into play. Even at quite high levels of domestic competition, it is often difficult to draw any other impression.

This is a great shame because, like tennis, the service has grown in significance in recent years to the point where it would not be an understatement to say that it is now the most important stroke.

At what other point in the game does a player have the opportunity to exercise complete control over the ball? A good service can win a point outright, it can open up the rally for an attacking shot, it can deceive the opponent and in some cases, it can even become a psychological threat to the receiver. You only have to look at the way in which the Chinese, and now several of the top European teams, have come to exploit its potential to realize what a valuable weapon it can be.

It makes good sense to impress upon any newcomer the advantages to be gained from being able to serve well. It doesn't mean that they have to be able to impart fantastic amounts of spin. Just simply that they are capable of delivering a tight, economical service which is strong enough to prevent the opponent from gaining an advantage.

The Service Laws

Because the service has been delivered in so many innovative and dramatic ways in the past, the ITTF has been forced to legislate on a number of successive occasions on the manner in which it should be delivered. In the 1950s when sponge rubber first came on to the scene, several of its early exponents started to gain what was seen as an unfair advantage by spinning the ball with their fingers prior to actually serving it. In the late seventies many combination bat players took to hiding the bat from the opponent's view by concealing it under the table immediately prior to the service. By doing this they gained a great deal of deception because the opponent would be unaware until the very last minute which side of the bat would be used to strike the ball and, therefore, whether it would be spinning or not. Other players hid both the ball and bat from view by standing with their backs to both the opponent and the umpire, turning only at the last second at the point of contact with the ball.

Umpires, therefore, now pay very close attention to whether a service conforms with the laws of the game. It is important that beginners should be aware of these laws and that they are capable of delivering a service which is not only effective but also legal and correct. The main rules to bear in mind are that:

• The service begins with the ball resting on the palm of the free hand which should be above the table, stationary and flat with the fingers together and the thumb free.
• The bat should begin the service action from above the table.
• The ball should be thrown upwards at least 16 centimetres.
• The ball should be struck on its descent, from behind the white baseline. It should bounce once on the server's side of the table before crossing the net.
• The service should at all times be clearly visible to the umpire.

On service, the ball must be thrown upwards from the palm of the hand. Note how the fingers are upturned very slightly making the palm into a shallow well in which the ball sits without rolling.

Learning to Serve

It is by no means easy for a beginner to coordinate all the actions that go into the service routine and at the same time stay within the laws of the game. A step-by-step approach is often the best way of achieving this and you might want to try the following method.

1. Start by getting the player used to holding the ball still in the palm of the hand without it rolling around. This is a common difficulty and it can be easily overcome by making the palm of the hand into a very shallow cup by slightly bending the knuckles.

2. Now move on to the throw up. To make sure the ball is being thrown upwards in a consistent vertical path, ask the player to position the bat directly beneath the free hand. A good throw up should result in the ball landing on the centre of the bat held directly below.

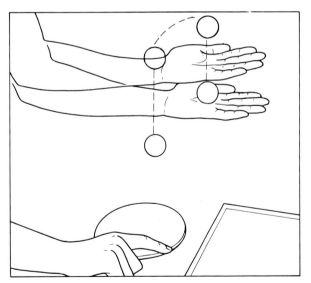

3. Next, instead of simply letting the ball bounce on the bat from the throw up, encourage the player to swing the bat a little as the ball is descending, hitting it up and forward over the net to bounce on the receiver's side. You might find the easiest way to introduce this stage is to adapt an existing technique, like the backhand push. If necessary, let the player lean over the table and gradually take the point of contact with the ball closer towards the baseline and finally just behind the baseline.

4. The last stage of the process is to adjust the swing a little so that the ball is being struck downwards making it bounce once on the server's side of the net before ultimately bouncing on the receiver's side.

It is important at all the stages outlined above that the bat is not being held too tightly. This will only restrict the player's ability to control the length of the service.

The second stage of learning to serve is to let the player drop the ball on to the bat and hit upwards on to the opponent's side of the table.

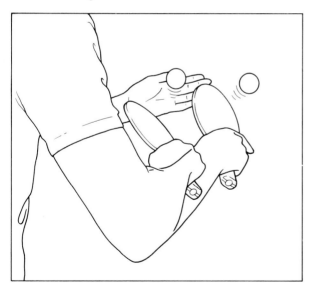

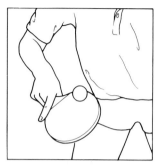

Brushing down the ball, with the bat held at an open angle should help to keep the service short.

What Makes a Safe Service a Good Service ?

Top players spend hours and hours serving endless balls across the table in a bid to perfect their serving technique. But, irrespective of experience or ability, there are a number of basic points that all players need to know and practise in order to coordinate the body actions involved to perform a basic legal service.

Many new players complain that the ball bounces too high when they serve, thereby giving the receiver the opportunity to drive it hard back at them. Others complain that they are unable to control the length of their services which vary constantly.

Let's examine the first point. The main factor influencing the height to which the ball bounces is the height at which contact between bat and ball is made in relation to the table. If the server is hitting the ball at say, 30 centimetres or so above the table, then the ball will bounce at almost the same height over the net. Ideally, players should be encouraged to make contact at roughly the same height as the net or somewhere between 15 and 20 centimetres.

Next, the question of the length of serve. Short, medium, and long services all have their place in today's game. Where the ball bounces on the receiver's side of the table depends to a great extent on where it is placed on the server's own side. For a short service, the ball should be played close to the net on the server's own side. A medium length service requires the ball to be played mid table, and a long service is most easily achieved when the ball is played close to the server's own baseline, if it is to bounce at an equivalent point on the receiver's side of the table.

Another factor to bear in mind when looking at the length of the service is the angle of the bat. For a short or medium length service, make sure that it moves downwards, brushing the underside of the ball. By doing this, an element of backspin will be imparted, making it that little bit more awkward for the receiver to create an opening with an attacking shot.

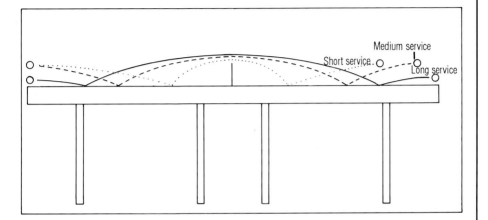

For a longer service, the bat needs to be closed a little, making contact with the back of the ball. Probably the most utilized service in the modern game is a short to medium length service down the centre of the table, directed at the receiver's playing shoulder. This has come to be known as the 'two bounce serve'. In other words, if there was no one to return the ball, it would bounce twice on the receiver's side with the second bounce on or about the baseline. The length and direction are just about right to make it difficult for the opponent to decide in the first instance whether to play a forehand or backhand shot and secondly, whether to simply push the ball back, or try to drive or flick it instead. With this length of service, it is also quite possible for the server to put a useful amount of sidespin on the ball which only adds to the receiver's problems.

The length of a service will depend very much on where it is placed on the server's own side of the table. For a short service, it should be made to bounce as close to the net as possible.

Receiving the Serve

Let us turn our attention now to the other side of the equation, that of returning or receiving the service. From a beginner's point of view there are essentially three points to consider:

• The stance and position of the receiver in relation to the server.
• How best to move to the ball, particularly when it is served short.
• What type of stroke to use to make the most effective return.

At no other point in the game does a correct stance become more vital. Make sure then, that the player is positioned square to the server, poised ready and alert to move swiftly into action. The bat should be pointing at the ball. (For the key factors on good stance, see Chapter 3). Remind him that inevitably the server's bat is going to make contact with the ball so there is no need to waste time following the throw-up of the ball. Just keep the eyes firmly fixed on the bat.

The position of the receiver will depend to a large extent from where the ball is being served. If it is coming from well over on the server's forehand side, then the receiver needs to be aware of the possible angles of play that need to be covered (see recovery positions in Chapter 5). In general terms, at least 50 to 60 per cent of play needs to be covered by the forehand, more so if the receiver has a useful forehand.

Long serves can be covered using the sort of stepping footwork we looked at in Chapter 5. As far as short or medium length serves are concerned, the golden rule is to move the nearest foot to the bounce of the ball. This should bring the head and body sufficiently close to the ball to enable good control to be exerted.

Lastly, the type of stroke to use will very much depend on the length and type of spin on the ball. A short backspin service is best received with a short delicate push over the net with the ball being taken just before the peak of its bounce. Make sure that the bat is not being gripped too tightly so that the desired level of touch is not lost. The medium or two bounce service can be returned with what is referred to as the flick - taking the ball at its peak and hitting it deep into the server's side of the table. This is similar in principle to the two basic drive shots discussed in Chapter 3. The

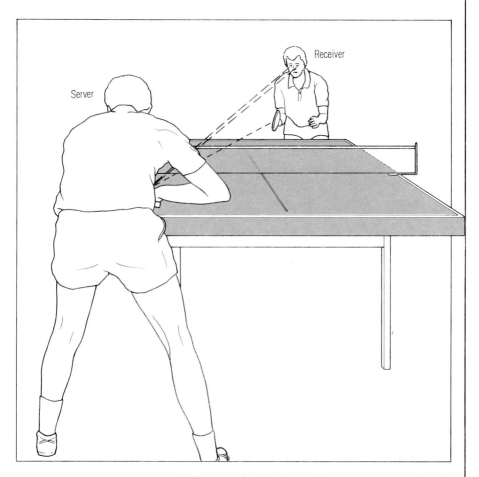

real difference is that it is played with a short arm where the wrist is the main moving joint, rotating quickly in a 'flicked' fashion over the back of the ball.

Long services should be dealt with using the forehand drive. By keeping the ball deep and into the server's body, it narrows the angle of play available. All these types of receive have one thing in common; they are positive. If the receiver dithers over the return it is a sure fire way of getting into difficulty.

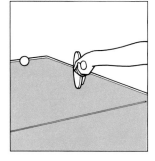

Forehand 'flick' return of service. Note how the wrist is cocked backwards ready to be snapped forwards at the point of contact with the ball.

Practising the Service and Receive

It is not easy for the coach to create practice situations which concentrate on the service and receive, without boredom on the part of the pupils quickly setting in. You need to be varied and imaginative but here are one or two exercises you might like to try. In the long run, though, hours of dedicated practice on the service, in particular, can pay handsome dividends and literally put points on a player's game almost overnight.

Exercise 1

The server serves five short backhand services and then five short forehand services into boxes 1,2 ,3 and 4. The services should be short enough so that they would be capable of bouncing twice on the receiver's side.

The receiver pushes the service into boxes 1 and 2 back into box 8, and then serves into boxes 3 and 4 into box 7.

The server then serves five long backhand services and then five long forehand services into box 5. The receiver returns each one into box 9, preferably by using a forehand drive.

Total 50 services

Server's end

Exercise 1

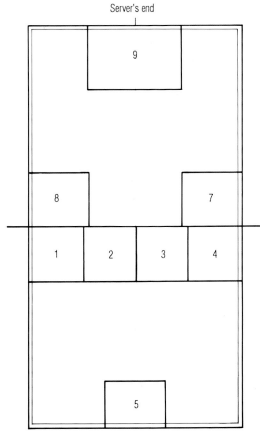

Receiver's end

Exercise 2

The server plays 50 services at random into the five boxes shown
on the diagram. The receiver tries to return as many as possible
deep into box 9 using attacking shots wherever possible.

Both these exercise can be made 'fun' games. For example, if the
server fails to hit any of the prescribed targets over the course of
50 services, each miss counts as one sit-up, star jump or squat
thrust. Equally, each time the receiver fails to return the ball into
the right area, a similar penalty applies. The penalty exercises
accumulated by both players are performed at the conclusion of
the exercise.

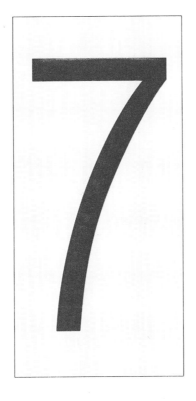

POWER PLAY

Power Play

If the basic strokes are the foundation of the beginner's game, it is the development of power that sees the transition of a beginner to a competitive player.

What is meant by power and why is it so important? As far as the table tennis player is concerned, power has two essential uses: to hit the ball harder and faster and to generate spin on the ball. You might argue that these are advanced techniques and not really the concern of someone learning the game. In a sense you are right but you will quickly find that the urge to hit the ball harder and attempt to spin it tends to occur remarkably early in a player's career. It's useful, therefore, to understand and appreciate the various factors which constitute the power-based game. It will also become immediately apparent from observing your player's first foray into competition that an ability to crack the ball hard when the opportunity arises is absolutely vital.

To understand how power is generated we must return to the seven technical points discussed in Chapter 3. Whether hitting the ball hard and fast or spinning it, the bat needs to be moving at considerable speed. We can achieve this by making adjustments to both the forehand and backhand drives in the following three departments.

Length

You will remember how in three basic forms of the two drive shots, the swing or length of the stroke is kept relatively short. This is so the player can maintain good control and keep the rally going with some degree of consistency. To speed the stroke up, the length of the swing needs to be increased.

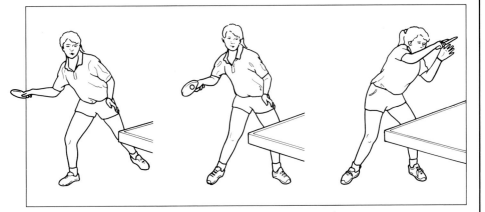

The fast forehand drive. To generate power, it is important that the player uses the whole of the body and transfers the weight from the right leg through to the left.

Body Action

Taking the forehand drive as an example, instead of simply using the waist and shoulders in the stroke, start earlier and lower in the body by using the legs as well. The knees should be bent and then pushed forwards, transferring the body weight from the back foot to the front foot. All this energy needs to be transmitted upwards, through the body and ultimately through to the bat itself. Power play involves using the whole of the body.

Bat Arm

All three joints in the arm play their part in helping the bat move speedily towards its collision course with the ball. In the basic forehand and backhand drive, we tend to use only one or two joints. In the power versions, it is vital that all three are synchronized together as part of the energy transmission process outlined above. If one of these joints is locked in some way, then this process will be prevented from taking place and speed will be lost. All must be fluid and free to move. The shoulder moves first, then the elbow starts to close and finally the wrist snaps through the ball.

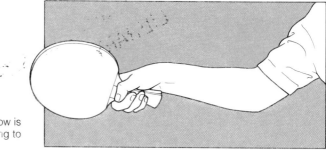

It is essential that the elbow is more extended when trying to drive through the ball.

The other point to bear in mind when looking at the bat arm, is the angle at the elbow. A long arm makes for a wider swing which in turn means a more powerful stroke.

A short arm, where the elbow is held in a position of say, 90° or so, is good for control but limits both forward movement of the arm and the arc of the swing. An angle of about 120° is better; any straighter than this and unless you are a world champion, it will be difficult, to say the least, to retain any real control or touch over the ball.

All these principles apply whether a player is learning to inject speed into the game or wants to put spin on the ball. The only real difference between speed and spin is the trajectory that the bat moves through when the ball is being struck. For speed the bat moves forward and through the back of the ball at the peak of its bounce. For spin, such as topspin, the bat tends to move upwards, brushing the back of the ball usually at a later stage in the bounce.

Spinning the ball is looked at in greater depth in the next chapter.

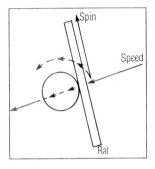

For speed alone, the bat needs to hit through the ball as shown by the 'speed' axis on the above diagram. Very little through movement is needed to generate spin. Instead, the bat must brush the ball with the bat moving downwards or as is shown here, in an upwards direction.

When to Introduce Power into a Player's Game

The answer to this question depends on your definition of a beginner. Anyone who has failed to master the basic strokes is in no position to progress to learning about how to hit the ball harder and, in this respect, power probably constitutes an advanced technique. Most coaches tend to find that newcomers to the game need around 60 hours playing time devoted solely to developing these basic techniques. During this period, it should also prove possible to introduce various footwork patterns as well as the service and receive. So, try not to fall into the typical trap of attempting to teach advanced skills before the basic game has become fully established. This will lead in the long term to serious flaws appearing in the player's game. Nevertheless, keep it in mind as the next logical step in the learning process.

The Forehand Smash

The only exception to the above advice is the smash. It's not unreasonable for any enthusiastic novice who has become relatively adept at the game to want to know how to kill the ball, finish the rally and therefore win the point.

The smash is invariably performed on the forehand wing and as with the forehand drive, the stance needs to be side to square. It is impossible to kill any ball you choose and the real art of the forehand smash lies in being able to single out the right opportunity. As a general rule, a ball with little or no spin on it, bouncing halfway down the table, and at a height noticeably greater than that of the net, would be an ideal candidate.

All the three factors we have just looked at need to be positioned correctly; the swing needs to be long, the shot must involve the whole body with the weight transferring emphatically from the back to front foot, and the bat arm needs to extend with a wide angle at the elbow. The real difference between, say, a fast forehand drive and a forehand kill is the trajectory that the bat

Forehand kill
The player must transmit all
the body weight down and
through the ball. Note how
the stroke starts with the bat
slightly above the height of
the ball.

moves through. In the kill, the bat should start above the height of the ball, which if possible, should be taken at the peak of its bounce. It moves in a downwards plane, in turn, hitting the ball violently down on to the other side of the table.

All the power and energy generated goes into hitting the ball forwards. No brushing or stroking action is involved. Many players make a mess of this shot because, more often than not, they start the stroke with the bat lower than the height of the ball. This results in them over-hitting the other side of the table.

A good way of perfecting the forehand kill is to set up a fun game for the players along the following lines. You will need a dozen or so balls and, as the coach, serve them with a reasonably high bounce but without spin in quick succession across the table to a player positioned at the other side. His role is to kill them all back at you. The rest of the players in the group must chase around behind you, gathering the balls, returning them to you so that you have a continuous supply to keep the player under pressure. Let each player take their turn giving each one about a minute or so each on killing the ball.

UNDERSTANDING SPIN

Understanding Spin

Whether you are a student coach, a keen school teacher or just a parent who has got roped into the game by enthusiastic offspring, it will be impossible to avoid an encounter with the game's most magical ingredient, spin. There is no other racquet sport where it has such a critical influence and unfortunately, it rears its ugly head at the earliest stages in most players' careers.

If you are working with beginners, it's not vital to be able to teach strokes which spin the ball. It is, however, helpful that you know how it occurs, what its effects are and perhaps more importantly, how to deal with it.

How is it Produced?

Spin has become a popular weapon in recent years because of the advances made in rubber technology which have increased the ability of the rubber surface to grip and spin the ball as contact is made. In technical terms, this is known as the 'co-efficient of friction', the same jargon used by tyre manufacturers assessing the ability of their products to grip the surface of the road. You can test a piece of bat rubber for grip simply by pushing the ball hard down on to the surface and then attempting to drag it across the bat. If it refuses to move, then the rubber is still in good condition. If it slides straight across the blade with only the slightest push then it is 'dead' and it's time to invest in a new sheet. Table tennis rubber does not have an infinite life-span and after a period of time and use it will begin to lose both its elasticity (or bounce) and its grip.

The ball is made to spin during its flight when it is struck in a brushing or slicing action. Instead of the bat hitting through the ball, where the energy of the shot is devoted exclusively to driving it forward, it rubs across it. Only a small part of the energy that goes into the stroke is then devoted to forward momentum, the majority is used to spin the ball on its axis. The diagram opposite illustrates this point.

A downward brushing action generates backspin or 'chop' as it is sometimes known.

Different Types of Spin

Two forms of spin dominate table tennis - backspin, sometimes referred to as 'chop', and favoured by many defensive players, and topspin, otherwise known as 'loop' and preferred by most attacking players.

Backspin is exactly what its name suggests; although the ball moves forward, it is actually spinning backwards on its axis. It is achieved by the bat brushing downwards across the underside of the ball.

It has the effect of making the ball sit up when it bounces instead of rolling forward in the usual fashion. Because of this, there is a tendency for players to mis-time the ball by hitting it slightly late or, more often than not, into the net. For a beginner, faced with a player who chops the ball, the easiest way to deal with it at this stage is to push the ball back making sure that the bat hits under the ball a little, lifting it up. Therefore, the bat angle need not be more open than usual. This prevents the spin from taking effect and making the ball skid down towards the net.

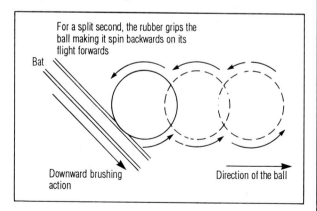

For a split second, the rubber grips the ball making it spin backwards on its flight forwards

Bat

Downward brushing action

Direction of the ball

An upward brushing action generates topspin or 'loop' as it is sometimes known.

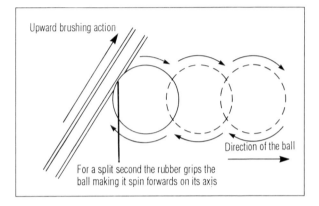

Upward brushing action

For a split second the rubber grips the ball making it spin forwards on its axis

Direction of the ball

Topspin is the exact opposite. It occurs when the bat brushes up the back of the ball, making it spin forward on its axis so it jumps forward suddenly on its bounce. The term loop came about because it describes the flight path of a ball with topspin on it. Initially the ball appears to move up but then suddenly loops and dips downwards over the net to the other side of the table.

The amount of topspin on a ball will very much depend on the manner in which the shot has been played. If virtually all the energy of the stroke has gone into brushing the ball late in its bounce as though the bat is like a knife trying to trim the skin of the apple in mid air, then it is odds on that the ball will be loaded with spin. This is certain if the stroke is executed with great speed, but results in the ball moving forward relatively slowly. If the ball is travelling fast and it looks as though it has been hit at the peak or before the peak of its bounce, then there will be much less topspin on it.

The best way for a beginner to deal with a topspin ball is to block it back. This is a technique which was mentioned briefly in

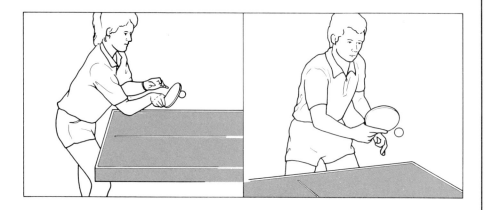

Chapter 4 which looked at the basic strokes. The basis for both a forehand and backhand block is the same as the drive, except that both the length of the shot and the bat arm are short and the ball is taken as soon as it bounces, very much like a half volley. This stops the ball from flying up off the receiver's bat. By taking the ball early with a closed bat, spin is prevented from taking full effect.

The forehand and backhand blocks, often used to counter the effects of topspin. In both cases, make sure the player takes the ball early in the bounce.

When blocking the ball, there is hardly any need for forward movement. Instead, feed off the spin and pace of the opponent and let the ball simply rebound off the bat. This is where feel and touch come into their own. If the bat is held too rigid or if the grip is too tight, the ability to control the spin and cushion the shot will be that much less.It almost goes without saying at this stage that it will be impossible to read any sort of spin if the player fails to watch the opponent's bat and its action on the ball. It also helps to watch the ball after it has been struck; if you can see the manufacturer's markings on the ball during its flight then it will not be spinning very much.

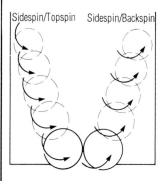

Sidespin/Topspin   Sidespin/Backspin

A ball can spin on its axis in many different directions. However, backspin or topspin will usually be the predominant spin.

Returning a Spin Service

Many players, particularly youngsters, become demoralized if they cannot return their opponent's service. Spin is exploited to its fullest in the service and receive so it's handy to know how to cope with it.

The service gives most players their best opportunity to put an element of sidespin on to the ball. This is a variation of the spin which we have not looked at so far but it is not as complex as it sounds. Both backspin and topspin balls can be produced with an element of sidespin at the same time. For example, in a sidespin chop, the ball will still be spinning backwards but on a slightly different axis. The same applies to the topspin. It all depends on the direction with which the bat brushes the ball.

As well as brushing the ball to topspin it, the bat can also brush to the side at the same time, thereby creating a form of topspin/sidespin. This will result in the ball jumping forwards but to one side when it bounces. A similar effect can be gained when brushing down the ball to backspin it.

When returning a sidespin serve, broadly the same techniques are used as when the player is responding to backspin or topspin during the course of a normal rally, with one or two slight adjustments.

Firstly, it's important to observe whether the server is brushing over the ball or under it. That will tell you whether the predominant spin is going to be topspin, which will need a closed bat angle to return, or backspin which will need an open bat angle. Then, try and establish to which side the ball is likely to bounce from watching the sideways direction that the bat is being swung in.

If the bat is being swung from the server's right to left (in which case it's probably a forehand serve assuming the server is right-handed), the sidespin will probably make the ball jump away from the receiver's bat to the receiver's right. To counteract this, the receiver should adjust the bat angle to aim for the opposite direction and return to the right.

If the bat is being swung from the server's left to right (in which case is is probably a backhand serve) the sidespin will probably make the ball jump off the receiver's bat to the receiver's left. Therefore, aim for the opposite direction and return to the right.

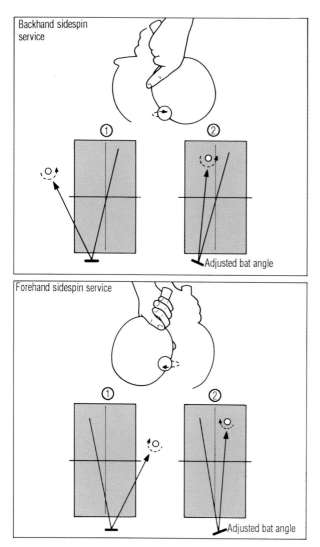

Backhand sidespin service

① ②

Adjusted bat angle

Forehand sidespin service

① ②

Adjusted bat angle

Make sure that the bat angle is adjusted sufficiently when receiving a sidespin service in order to prevent the ball flying off the table altogether.

Beginners and Spin

This chapter has dealt with the dynamics of spin , its importance in today's game and ways in which to respond to the threat it poses. There has been no guidance on how to generate strokes which impart spin.

This is deliberate in some ways, because this is a book which is concerned with the coaching of the beginner or inexperienced player and producing spin is a sophisticated and advanced technique. Most players need to be at a stage where control, consistency and accuracy are almost second nature. Until these basic attributes are acquired, it is unlikely that the newcomer to the game will have developed the touch or dexterity needed to be able to make the ball spin to any significant degree.

The next logical stage is to develop pace and power to move the ball around more quickly. If you try and teach spin before this has been achieved, there's a great possibility that you might spoil later development. This is because spin usually involves a variation in the timing point. On many topspin strokes, the ball is taken after the peak of the bounce. Your job as coach is initially to instil in the player a timing point for a shot which takes the ball at the peak of the bounce. Only by hitting the ball at this point will he be able to develop a game of speed and power. If a player learns to spin the ball too early in his career, he may never be able to drive it hard because he is using a later timing point which will become hard to vary.

GETTING FIT TO PLAY

Getting Fit to Play

Warming Up

Cold weather affects table tennis players in much the same way as it affects the average family saloon. In order to perform to full efficiency, the average player needs to be warmed up first, just as you would warm up a car's engine before setting off to work in the morning. Players need coordination, flexibility and touch and these are attributes which cannot be instantly switched on and off like a light bulb.

In order to get the best out of your performers, it makes sense to start off the coaching session with some form of off-the-table warm up. As far as a match is concerned, failure to warm up beforehand can mean the difference between winning and losing. Even with raw beginners, there's much to be said for getting into the habit of including a warm-up period as an established part of the session. Although the risk of injury at this level is marginal, a good warm up will both stretch and loosen the muscles. In a cold and draughty gym, it can be a way of bringing the body's temperature up to its normal level.

A simple warm-up session usually consists of two parts; general exercises for the whole body followed by flexibility exercises concentrated on the muscle groups used most during play.

Here are some warm-up programmes you might wish to try. By no means are they exhaustive or the definitive way of conducting a warm-up - it's up to you to make alterations and additions as you see fit. Try and encourage the players to keep tracksuits or sweatshirt tops on during the initial stages of the routine in order to maintain body heat and maximize the effect of the warm-up process.

General Body Exercises

When there is plenty of room
• Jog slowly around the room (1 minute)
• Skip around the room (1 minute)
• Run backwards around the room (30 seconds)
• Skip sideways around the room (30 seconds)
• Run and catch the person in front (20 seconds)
• Return to jogging slowly but changing directions when instructed by the coach (30 seconds)
• Finish
Total time approximately 4 minutes

If space is limited
• Jog slowly on the spot (30 seconds)
• Change to running slowly on the toes (20 seconds)
• Return to jogging on the spot (15 seconds)
• Ten knee to chest jumps
• Return to jogging (15 seconds)
• Eight squat thrusts
• Return to jogging (15 seconds)
• Six sit ups
• Return to jogging (15 seconds)
• Four start jumps
• Return to jogging (15 seconds)
• Quick arm rolling (15 seconds in each direction)
Total time approximately 5 minutes

Knee bends

Flexibilty routines to follow straight after a general exercise routine, starting with the head and moving down the body:
• Roll the neck in wide circles, clockwise and anti-clockwise for 30 seconds
• Arm circles, clockwise and anti-clockwise for 30 seconds
• Elbow circles, clockwise and anti-clockwise for 20 seconds (loosens elbows)
• Vertical arm stretching for 20 seconds
• Hip rotation in wide circles, clockwise and anti-clockwise for 30 seconds (for lower back)
• Toe touching, legs wide and straight for 10 seconds each leg (for hamstrings and waist)
• Knee rotation, in wide circles clockwise and anti-clockwise for 20 seconds (for knee joints)
• Ankle and wrist rolling simultaneously for 20 seconds
Total time approximately 3 minutes

Before sending the players on to the tables make sure that their breathing is back to normal.

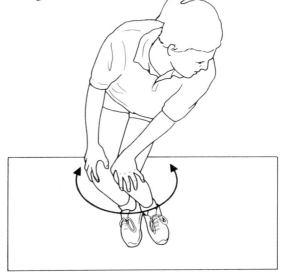

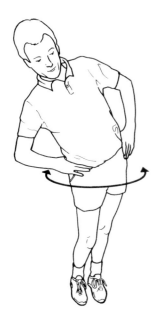

Hip rotation (left) and ankle and wrist rolling (right)

General Fitness

From the beginner's point of view, the physical demands made by table tennis are few. Of greater concern are the dynamics involved in simply hitting the ball over the net, and the worst injury the player can sustain in the early days is a bad back from continually having to pick the ball up off the floor. But as consistency begins to emerge and the ball stays on the table longer, more physical exertion is involved. It soon becomes apparent that there is a need for some level of physical fitness.

Take, for example, a promising young player who wishes to develop a game based around a powerful forehand drive. The energy involved in hitting, say 20 to 30 hard, continuous drives from various parts of the table is quite significant. This shot uses the strength in the upper legs which in turn are big consumers of oxygen. Cardio-vascular endurance or stamina, as it is more popularly known, is vital, as is muscular endurance.

In developing a training programme, we have to think both in terms of it being specific not only to the game of table tennis but also to the style of the player in question. One of the best ways of recreating the physical demands that certain styles of play involve, is by using shadow play to supplement the table practice routines. Other typical exercises would be 'bunny hops' as well as fast, sideways steps between points approximately three metres apart and short distance, fast sprints.

Even for accomplished players, off-the-table training programmes are the exception rather than the rule. Too much emphasis on physical training can be a total waste of time. All the stamina, strength and endurance necessary can be incorporated into shadow play or actual on-the-table exercises once a good level of consistency has been attained.

PLANNING AND RUNNING A SESSION

Planning and Running a Session

It's your first coaching session tomorrow night! Is everything ready? Presumably you've sorted out the venue. And, of course, the players know at what time to report. Have they got their own bats or are you providing them? What about tables, nets and balls ... are there enough? What are you going to talk about? Have you ironed your kit? There are so many things to remember, you wonder how you are going to get through.

Relax! The straightforward solution to your dilemma is preparation. Let's take a look at the things you should have taken care of before you even set foot in the venue.

If tables are in short supply, a temporary solution can be achieved. Eight players can usefully occupy one table if they are positioned as shown in the diagram below.

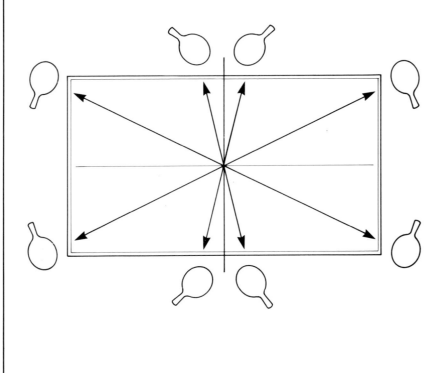

How many players?

The number of players you accommodate in one session will depend very much on the number of tables you have at your disposal and your own limitations. As a rule, be wary of compromising the quality of your session by the quantity of your pupils. To make any real coaching progress and to ensure that you don't end up running a large-scale child minding operation, you would be well advised to take on board no more than eight pupils. Therefore, it would be ideal if you had four tables at your disposal, because this would then give you two players on each table. Unfortunately, we don't live in an ideal world so if you have only three tables, you will have to double up on one.

Sustaining interest is everything. Youngsters, in particular, want to spend as much time on the table as possible so they won't be thrilled at the idea of having to wait for their turn to have a go. Don't forget, you will probably be in competition with several other sports and young people will quickly take their custom elsewhere if they are bored with what you have on offer.

How old?

Beginners come in all shapes, sizes ... and ages. Young people are generally more receptive to tuition than adults and they learn more quickly. Most Chinese youngsters start playing at the age of seven or eight and in some cases at five and six. You need to bear in mind, however, that the inherent ability to control the ball is usually less developed in someone of this age than in a youngster of eleven or twelve years of age. In any event, try and keep an even standard of abilities. Pairing a more experienced player with a total novice results in disappointment for both parties.

Session Planning

Few coaches are gifted enough to walk into a session and run the whole event straight off the top of their heads. This doesn't mean to say that most people don't try from time to time, but the result is usually disappointing, particularly for the players. You should have a good idea of the ground you want to cover in advance. A few minutes set aside to scribble some notes beforehand pays dividends in the long run.

A typical coaching session would follow this sort of pattern

1. Warm up to loosen muscles and joints (7-10 minutes).
2. Knock up to activate hand-eye coordination and touch (5 minutes).
3. Introduction to outline the programme for the session (3 minutes).
4. Demonstration to provide the players with a visual representation of the technique (3 minutes).
5. Analyze the player's performance of the technique and suggest corrections (10 minutes)
6. Develop various exercises based around the technique, using regular patterns (for improvers, this stage could be supplemented by irregular patterns) and conditional play (20 to 30 minutes).
7. Finish with match play (10 to 15 minutes).

Total time 1 to 1 hour and 15 minutes

This would be a typical framework around which a session for either beginners or improvers could be planned. Let's consider each area in turn in a little more detail and see what is involved.

Warm up and Knock up

The importance of a good warm up was covered in Chapter 9 and even if you are working with total beginners, warming up is a habit you should get them into from day one. It is often useful if you explain the reasons for the warm-up to the players. The brief knock-up on the tables which follows is really an extension of the

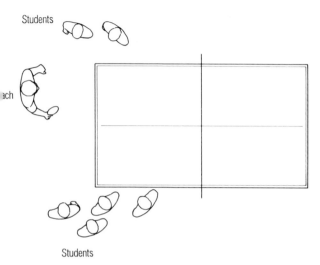

Students

ach

Students

Make sure the demonstration is visible in its entirety to all the students in your group.

warm-up process. Obviously, for someone who has never played before, it is unnecessary, but as the weeks roll by, let the players get the feel of the ball before the main part of the session commences. The whole of the warm-up/knock-up phase need take no longer than ten to 12 minutes.

Introducing the Theme of the Session

For total newcomers to the sport, the first thing you introduce is yourself. Follow this by finding out who the members of your group are. Someone who has never played before will need to know how to hold the bat correctly before you let them near the table. This might also be an opportune moment to include a few words about the various types of bat that are available. Speak clearly, avoid using jargon and make sure that everyone can hear you.

More often than not, you will need to demonstrate a given technique and for many student coaches this is an area which causes most concern. Firstly, it's not always necessary to demonstrate a stroke with the ball in play. A dry land or shadow play demonstration will often do and, in most cases, is better. It allows you the time to talk through the key points that you want to get across. If you don't feel confident enough to do that, don't worry, all is not lost. If possible, use an experienced and technically sound player as your model instead.

No matter what form of demonstration you eventually opt for, make sure that everyone can see the stroke in its totality, from the feet upwards. Also remember that there may be left-handers in the group so don't forget to allow for this, particularly when talking about footwork patterns. If you propose to demonstrate a stroke, position the group in the manner shown on page 99.

It's not sufficient for the players to watch you from the other side of the net. From this vantage point, they are unable to see the full extent of the stance and how the feet are positioned.

Keep your introduction and demonstration as brief as possible. If it's strokeplay that you are considering, it will be very difficult to get across all seven of the main characteristics of a particular shot all in one go. Just pick out two or three of the more important points, for example, bat arm and angle, stance and timing point. Build in the remainder at later stages during the session. Remember, it's time on the table that's important and the players haven't come along just to hear you ramble on all night!

Analyze Performance

Put the players back on to the tables and let them try out the shot. Spend a few minutes or so analyzing each player's technique using the seven point framework as your checklist. Pick out the typical faults which are common to a number of individuals and, if necessary, stop the session briefly and explain how to correct them.

Alternatively, you may feel that it's more important to go round each player in turn and make corrections individually. Undoubtedly, one of the most effective ways of analyzing anyone's performance of a given technique is by using video. If you have this facility at your disposal, by all means use it. Remember, however, to allow for the extra time involved in recording and playback. Because of this, video usually comes into its own when coaching on a one-to-one basis as opposed to a group.

As the practice develops and the technique begins to emerge, add in the remainder of your key points, for example, the correct use of the free arm or emphasize the need to maintain the right sort of stance throughout the rally.

Don't be afraid to praise a good effort in order to boost someone's confidence; you will probably find that the players respond warmly to your enthusiasm.

Developing the Practice

Boredom will quickly set in if you confine the practice to exactly the same exercise for 20 minutes or so. This is where a little advance planning comes in handy because you will have thought up suitable variations beforehand, designed to develop and enhance your theme for the session. If you do take the trouble to devise a plan, use it as a framework and not as a tablet of stone which needs to be adhered to rigidly. The key to a worthwhile and enjoyable session lies in how easily you can adjust or amend your plans to meet changing circumstances.

For example, you should try to ensure that you have contingency plans up your sleeve in the event of a player not turning up or discovering that you have one table less than you originally anticipated. You may also find that a certain exercise you had intended to include is not entirely suitable, in which case, delete it from your plan and substitute something different. Also, remember to mix the players around to avoid them playing with the same partner for prolonged periods. Although you don't want to bore the talented player, it's equally important that you don't rush the slow learner.

Conditional Play or Games

The next logical stage in a coaching session is to introduce some competitive element which falls short of actual matchplay. You can do this in a number of ways. For players who have gone past the stage of being a raw beginner to what is best described as an improver, one of the best methods is by using conditional play.

Conditional play is when the player has constraints imposed within a given practice situation. For example, only being able to play within a certain portion of the table, or only being able to play forehand shots or perhaps having to win the point within seven balls. To give the players a bit of fun and an added incentive to meet your conditions, impose penalties of five sit-ups or ten star-jumps if they fail to meet the targets set. Be careful, though, to ensure that your targets are realistic and that you aren't always penalizing the same few individuals. If this is so, handicap the more accomplished in order to restore the status quo.

For raw beginners, the sort of conditional play described above may be too advanced or simply inappropriate. Instead, there's no harm in injecting a little levity into the proceedings by organizing a fun game.

We touched on one or two of these in Chapter 4 which dealt with the four basic strokes. Several more ideas for fun games are set out at the end of this chapter.

Matchplay

Matchplay is the concluding activity of a session, although it will take a couple of weeks before you are in a position to incorporate it into a beginners' course. More often than not, youngsters will welcome the excitement of being given an outlet for their competitive instincts.

A good way of giving each player a wide selection of opponents during this phase is to organize the matches on a 'winner moves up, losers move down' basis. Number your tables from one upwards. When you give the command 'play', everyone starts their match simultaneously. As soon as one of the contests reaches 15 in the score, the player who is winning shouts to everyone else to stop playing. Irrespective of the score on the adjoining tables, play stops immediately and all those players who are winning at this point move up to the next table and those who are losing move downwards.

One of the great advantages of organizing the matchplay phase on this basis is that it saves you the inconvenience of having to repeatedly pair contestants. It also ensures constant, uninterrupted participation. Players who might be trailing in their matches will be chasing around frantically to retrieve the ball and resume play as soon as possible in the hope of redressing the balance. An interesting variation on this exercise is to adjust the rules slightly, so that the players serve alternately for the first five points, whereupon whoever is leading retains the service for the remainder of the game.

How Long should the Session Last ?

The duration of any coaching session will be governed by both the attention span and the responsiveness of the players. For total beginners, as a general rule of thumb, a session should last no longer than an hour to an hour and a quarter. By all means experiment with this suggested timespan but bear in mind that it's better to stop while enthusiasm is running high, than reach a stage where tiredness and boredom creep in.

For improvers, an hour and a half to two hours of intensive coaching is probably sufficient. Both players and coach need to be aware of the distinction between coaching and practise. During coaching we are looking at a process which involves learning, analyzing and correcting techniques. The players should absorb this information and take it away with them to apply and assimilate during practise sessions. Practice serves a different purpose and presents the player with the opportunity to 'groove' in a technique which may have been covered in previous coaching sessions. It goes without saying, therefore, that for real improvement to occur, particularly to gain consistency and accuracy, coaching must be continually supplemented by practice.

Sample Sessions

What follows are three examples of coaching sessions, one for a new group of complete beginners; one for a group of improvers who have been playing perhaps six months or so; and lastly, a session for players who have been playing for twelve to eighteen months or more.

Beginner's session
1. Warm-up (5-7 minutes).
2. Introduction to the theme of the evening which could be the grip, the basic ball skills and the backhand push. Demonstrate the correct grip (5 minutes).
3. Analyze performance by setting a simple exercise, such as bouncing the ball on one side of the bat, on alternate sides of the bat and the edge of the bat. Make adjustments where necessary to improve control, for example, keep the arm short and encourage the players to maintain a relaxed grip so they are able to feel the bounce of the ball. Develop the practice by giving the players a target to aim for, such as ten consecutive balls, then 15 and so on - play a fun game like a relay.

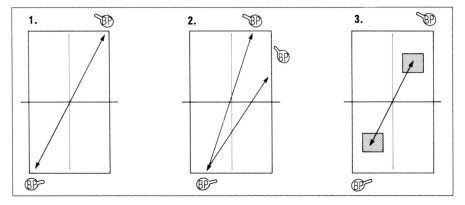

4. Demonstrate the backhand push as this will give the opportunity to explain the main points involved in a good stance and emphasize their importance. Move on to demonstrate the stroke itself.

5. Analyze performance of the back hand push and give each player feedback on their technique.

6. Develop various exercises (like those above)

7. Finish with another fun game based on the backhand push, such as 'Runaround' (see the section at the end of this chapter for a description).

Improvers' session

1. Warm up (7 minutes).

2. Knock up (5 minutes).

3. Introduction to the theme of the session, for example, improving footwork. Start by demonstrating stepping footwork when moving to the ball, from one side of the table to the other.

4. Analyze performance of a simple exercise routine where one player acts as a feeder and uses a backhand block to place the ball alternately to positions one metre apart. Using stepping footwork, the opposing player returns each ball with a forehand drive. Observe both technique and movement and make improvements where necessary. Reverse the player's roles and repeat the analysis.

Exercise 1 is a straightforward backhand push (BP) to backhand push (BP) using the diagonal. Exercise 2 involves on e player playing the ball alternatively to two different positions on the partner's backhand wing. Remember to reverse the exercise so that both players perform both tasks. Exercise 3 uses target areas to develop accuracy and consistency.

Stages 3 and 4 should occupy 10 minutes, 25-30 minutes should be allocated to stages 5 and 6 with the remainder of the session spent on 7.

Exercise 1 involves both players playing forehand drives with one playing the ball alternately to each wing of the table. Remember to reverse the practice so that each player performs both tasks. Exercise 2 requires three players per table, one player acts as controller and plays only a forehand block (FB). One of the other two must play one backhand drive (BD) and two forehand drives (FD) and move out from the table, during which time his partner has moved in to play the same three shots. Repeat. Exercise 3 is a game of 21 up but using only one side of the table. Furthermore, one player must use only a backhand block (BB) while his partner must use only a forehand drive (FD). Points are awarded against players if they play outside the prescribed area.

5. Develop various exercises (the following diagrams give some suggestions).
6. Matchplay.

Advanced improvers' session

1. Warm up (10 minutes).
2. Knock up (5 minutes).
3. Introduction to the theme of the session, for example, 'improving anticipation'. Start by explaining to the group the key factors which affect anticipation, (these are covered in Chapter 5, which looks at footwork, recovery and reaction). Give demonstrations of the stance and recovery positions and the importance of watching the opponent's body action and not just the ball.
4. Analyze performance in a semi-irregular exercise routine. One player, the feeder, forehand drives the ball to a backhand block return, using the backhand diagonal. The feeder may switch the ball wide to the other player's forehand at any point during the rally but shouts 'switch!' at the same time. Observe the technique of the player under examination, check that the correct footwork pattern is brought into use and that the stance is right and the player is clearly watching the body action of the opponent. After a while, alter the exercise by removing the shout 'switch', which has so far acted as a clue. Reverse the players roles and repeat the analysis.
5. Develop various exercises. The diagrams will give a few ideas.
6. Matchplay

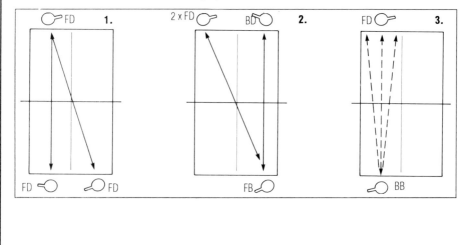

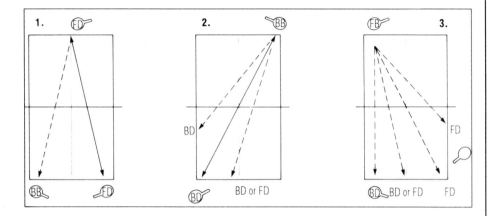

Further Ideas for Fun Games

Simple ball control games

Overtaking

Whilst bouncing the ball on the bat, the players run round the room with the aim of overtaking one another. Those players who are overtaken, or who drop the ball, drop out of the game.

Relays

With a minimum of two players in each team, bouncing the ball on the bat throughout. The race can be varied by making the players run in between a line of chairs or between the tables. Ensure that no one handles the ball when it is exchanged between team members.

All three exercises shown above involve the line of play being altered at random during the rally and this is shown by the dotted lines. Remember to reverse each routine so that both players have the opportunity to act as the 'controller'.

Runaround game

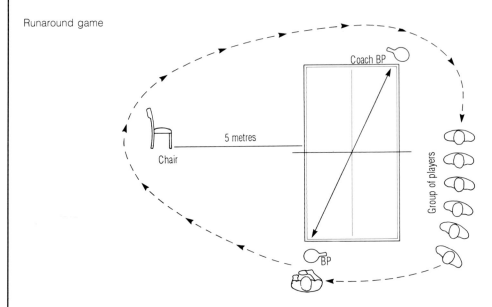

Relays
With a minimum of two players in each team, bouncing the ball on the bat throughout. The race can be varied by making the players run in between a line of chairs or between the tables. Ensure that no one handles the ball when it is exchanged between team members.

Runaround
Each player in turn plays a backhand push to a feeder and then runs around to the other side of the table. They must, however, first run around a chair positioned several yards to one side before rejoining the remainder of the players.

Give each player three lives, which are lost when they fail to make a clean return. Once these are exhausted the players drop out of the game, gradually reducing the number of running

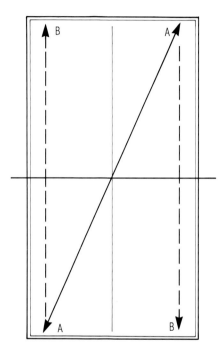

Football game

participants. The winner is the last remaining player (when the game gets down to two or three players reduce the distance travelled between shots by bringing the chairs closer or eventually removing them). This game could be used as a warm -up routine for a group of beginners.

More Difficult Fun Games

Cricket

This is a game designed to enhance the forehand smash and kill. Split the group into two teams of three or more, one elects to bowl and the other to bat. The bowler must toss the ball underarm to the other side of the table where it must bounce at at least head height. The batsman's aim is to return the ball with a smash. A run is scored if having made successful contact with the opposite side of the table, the ball eventually falls to the floor.

The fielders forming the bowling team must aim to catch the ball before it does so, in which case the batsman is 'out'. A wicket is also taken when a batsman drives the ball into the net or off the end of the table more than three times.

No balls (to be decided by the coach in charge) count as one run.

Team Singles

This requires a minimum of two players in each team. As soon as a player loses a point he or she is replaced with a colleague.

Football

Played in teams of two, one pair, Team A, stroke the ball to one another across the diagonal. At random, as a player sees a suitable opportunity, he smashes the ball down the line. If any of the opposing pair, Team B, fail to return it, a goal is scored. Eleven goals wins the match.

Games designed to improve consistency

1. The first table to achieve a continuous rally of say ten, 20, 30 and so on on successive strokes. The players on the losing tables must perform ten sit-ups, star jumps, or squat thrusts as penalties.

2. The table to sustain the longest rally based around a given stroke. Each table must start simultaneously and as soon as the ball goes out of play, the table in question must stop to allow the remaining tables to continue and a winner to emerge.

3. To improve consistency and speed, let each table compete to see how many strokes can be played without a mistake over a period of 30 seconds, then 45 seconds and so on.

11

COMPETITION

Competition

So far we have concentrated on the techniques and physical skills which beginners learn and acquire through coaching, enabling them to take part and hopefully enjoy the game. But there comes a point when all these attributes must be put to the test, and this occurs during competition. This is the stage when you, as a coach, discover that, despite all the best laid plans, your prospect's game collapses into ruin as soon as the umpire says 'love all'. In this chapter, we shall examine in simple terms the psychology and tactics of competition. In many respects, the two areas are closely connected as both have a significant impact on the performance and the capacity of the player to exploit his natural ability to its fullest extent.

Psychology

Table tennis is a sport which is practised by many players who possess all the natural ability in the world, but who have failed at the last hurdle because they were over anxious about competing. On the other hand, there are also many fine examples of less talented individuals who have exploited their more limited ability to its fullest potential and achieved considerable success. This could be attributed to their natural competitive instinct and a self-confidence which enables them to cope with the pressures that competition can present.

Clearly, therefore, one of the greatest challenges facing any coach is that of turning anxiety into self-confidence. Sports psychologists will tell you that the distortion produced by excessive psychological arousal will be most pronounced in those sports which require fine control or touch. Of course, table tennis is such a sport. What can you do to counter the effects of anxiety?

One technique which has been employed with noticeable success in a wide number of sports is goal setting. In order to gain any real effect, it is especially important that you are fully familiar with the personalities of the players with whom you are working. It also presupposes that you have gained a good appreciation of their respective levels of ability. The technique works by setting the individual achievable targets and this can take place within the context of a coaching session as well as within a match.

For example, you could set a beginner a simple target of 25 consecutive forehand drives during practise. A developing, attacking player could be set a target of trying to win each point within seven balls during the matchplay practice that takes place during a coaching session. Transposing this technique into the competitive arena, the goal does not have to be confined to winning, particularly if the opponent is stronger. Instead, it should be the aim of achieving the same target as that previously set during coaching, irrespective of whether the match is lost or won. The important point to remember throughout the whole process is that the player needs to accept that the target set is an achievable one and within his grasp.

Winning and losing should not be all-consuming. Building up a series of goals, which gradually increase in difficulty, and where the main emphasis is not that of winning at all cost can help a player make a steady transition from being not just a good practice partner, but a serious contender.

There are other ways of tackling the problem of acute anxiety, for example, re-structuring a coaching session in such a way, that the theme of competition is common to every exercise undertaken. Use irregular practises and conditional play constructed within a competitive framework, whereby a player can use only forehand drive stroke or where points can only be won from one's own service, as in badminton. The former might be useful in impressing upon a player with a strong forehand and nimble footwork, the value of that shot in a match or tournament, particularly if he frequently fails to exploit opportunities during competition. The latter might also be employed as a means of strengthening confidence and convincing some players of the importance of a strong, positive receive of service.

In most cases, worry or anxiety stems from a fear of losing. It is important that you as a coach are aware of the reasons for this. The root of the problem may lie in a misplaced desire to retain the credibility of a peer group such as fellow players or friends. Alternatively, it may lie in parental pressure to succeed and the inevitable worry of letting them down. On the other hand, it may be a concern that by losing, the player has let you down as the coach.

Clearly, it is important that you are capable of discussing the issue in an honest, open way so as to establish the cause, before attempting to remove the obstacle from the player's mind. Persuasion and encouragement will play an important part in this process - shouting at someone to concentrate or over-emphasis on the negative aspects of their game will invariably do more harm than good.

It's better to approach the situation from the point of view that 'doing your best' is more important than winning or losing. After all, your ultimate aim as a coach is to maximize a player's performance within the limits of his or her potential, irrespective of the result. If you achieve this, you have both succeeded.

Tactics

At a beginner's level, tactics have a relatively minor bearing in deciding the outcome of a match. Technique and skill are the factors which most often determine the final result. However, if the players in question are of similar standards and ability, then a basic tactical awareness can be a valuable asset. For some players this is instinctive and they require only minimal guidance in spotting an opponent's weaknesses before exploiting them to maximum effect. The great majority, however, are not blessed with such natural intuition.

Here are a few tactical tips that should come in handy for players new to competitive table tennis.

1. Try to arrange some immediate prematch practice, preferably on the same day, an hour or so before the match is due to start. Also, ensure that the player is fully warmed up beforehand.
2. Know your opponent. Use every opportunity to study the opposition before the match starts. Identify strengths and weaknesses, look at footwork and the ability to deal adequately with spin. The prematch knock up often provides a good chance to weigh up the opponent.

The area of indecision

Playing the ball to the opponent's shoulder often forces them into an awkward position.

3. Try and discourage the player from disclosing his stronger shots during the prematch knock up. These should be saved for the contest itself to spring an early surprise on the opponent.

4. Encourage a player to exploit the opponent's area of indecision. This is when the ball is played in such a position that the opponent must make a conscious decision between using the forehand and backhand stroke and can wind up playing a loose return instead. In most cases, the spot to aim for is the shoulder of the playing arm.

5. Play to weaknesses not to strengths. Obvious, maybe, but you would be amazed at the number of players who do anything but this. It's only when they are seven points down that it starts to dawn on them that something is going wrong. The best opportunity to exploit weaknesses often presents itself with the service and attacking the return - known as the third ball.

6. Encourage a player to be positive throughout the game. Half-hearted shots will not be sufficient, particularly when receiving service.

7. Lastly, luck. You make your own luck in this game so it's no good getting upset if the opposition seems to be getting more nets and edges than usual.

12

RULES OF THE GAME

RULES OF TABLE TENNIS

THE FOLLOWING ARE SELECTED EXTRACTS FROM THE RULES PUBLISHED BY THE INTERNATIONAL TABLE TENNIS FEDERATION.

3.1 The Table

3.1.1 The upper surface of the table, known as the 'playing surface', shall be rectangular, 2.74m long and 1.525m wide, and shall lie in horizontal plane 76cm above the floor.

3.1.2 The playing surface shall include the top edges of the table but not the sides of the table below the edges.

3.1.3 The playing surface may be of any material and shall yield a uniform bounce of about 23cm when a standard ball is dropped on to it from a height of 30cm.

3.1.4 The playing surface shall be uniformly dark coloured and matt, but with a white 'side line', 2cm wide, along each 2.74m edge and a white 'end line', 2cm wide, along each 1.525m edge.

3.1.5 The playing surface shall be divided into two equal 'courts' by a vertical net running parallel with the end lines, and shall be continuous over the whole area of each court.

3.1.6 For doubles, each court shall be divided into two equal 'half-courts' by a white 'centre-line', 3mm wide, running parallel with the side lines; the centre line shall be regarded as part of each right half-court.

3.2 The Net Assembly

3.2.1 The net assembly shall consist of the net, its suspension and the supporting posts.

3.2.2 The net shall be suspended by a cord attached at each end to an upright post 15.25cm high, the outside limits of the post being 15.25cm outside the side line.

3.2.3 The top of the net, along its whole length, shall be 15.25cm above the playing surface.

3.2.4 The bottom of the net, along its whole length, shall be as close as possible to the playing surface and the ends of the net shall be as close as possible to the supporting posts.

3.3 The Ball

3.3.1 The ball shall be spherical, with a diameter of 38mm.

3.3.2 The ball shall weigh 2.5gm.

3.3.3 The ball shall be made of celluloid or similar plastics material and shall be white or yellow, and matt.

3.4 The Racket

3.4.1 The racket shall be of any size, shape or weight but the blade shall be flat and rigid.
3.4.1.1 At least 85% of the blade by thickness shall be of natural wood.
3.4.1.2 An adhesive layer within the blade may be reinforced with fibrous material such as carbon fibre, glass fibre or compressed paper, but shall not be thicker than 7.5% of the total thickness or 0.35mm, whichever is the smaller.

3.4.2 A side of the blade used for striking the ball shall be covered with either ordinary pimpled rubber with pimples outwards having a total thickness including adhesive of not more than 2mm, or sandwich rubber with pimples inwards or outwards having a total thickness including adhesive of not more than 4mm.

3.4.2.1 'Ordinary pimpled rubber' is a single layer of non-cellular rubber, natural or synthetic, with pimples evenly distributed over its surface at a density of not less than 10/sq cm and not more than 50/sq cm.

3.4.3 The covering material shall extend up to but not beyond the limits of the blade, except that the part nearest the handle and gripped by the fingers may be left uncovered or covered with any material.

3.4.4 The blade, any layer within the blade and any layer of covering material or adhesive shall be continuous and of even thickness.

3.4.5 The surface of the covering material on a side of the blade or of a side of the blade if it is left uncovered, shall be uniformly darkcoloured and matt; any trimming round the edge of the blade shall be matt and no part of it shall be white.

3.4.6 Slight deviations from continuity of surface or uniformity of colour due to accidental damage, wear or fading may be allowed provided that they do not significantly change the characteristics of the surface.

3.4.7 At the start of a match and whenever he changes his racket during a match a player shall show his opponent and the umpire the racket he is about to use and shall allow them to examine it.

3.5 Definitions

3.5.1 A 'rally' is the period during which the ball is in play.

3.5.2 A 'let' is a rally of which the result is not scored.

3.5.3 A 'point' is a rally of which the result is scored.

3.5.4 The 'racket-hand is the hand carrying the racket.

3.5.6 A player 'strikes' the ball if he touches it with his racket, held in the hand, or with his racket-hand below the wrist.

3.5.7 A player 'volleys' the ball if he strikes it in play when it has not touched his court since last being struck by his opponent.

3.5.8 A player 'obstructs' the ball if he, or anything he wears or carries, touches it in play when it has not passed over the table or an imaginary extension of his end line, not having touched his court since last being struck by his opponent.

3.5.9 The 'server' is the player due to strike the ball first in the rally.

3.5.10 The 'receiver' is the player due to strike the ball second in a rally.

3.5.11 The 'umpire' is the person appointed to decide the result of each rally.

3.5.12 Anything that a player 'wears or carries' includes anything that he was wearing or carrying at the start of the rally.

3.5.13 The ball shall be regarded as passing 'over or around' the net if it passes under or outside the projection of the net assembly outside the table, or if, in a return, it is struck after it has bounced back over the net.

3.6 A Good Service

3.6.1 Service shall begin with the ball resting on the palm of the free hand, which shall be stationary, open and flat, with the fingers together and the thumb free.

3.6.2 The free hand, while in contact with the ball in service, shall at all times be above the level of the playing surface.

3.6.3 The whole of the racket shall be above the level of the playing surface from the last moment at which the ball is stationary on the palm of the free hand until the ball struck in service.

3.6.4 The server shall then project the ball, by hand only and without imparting spin, so that it rises at least 16cm after leaving the palm of the free hand.

3.6.5 As the ball is falling from the highest point of its trajectory the server shall strike it so that:
3.6.5.1 in singles, it touches first his court and then, passing directly over or around the net assembly, touches the receiver's court;
3.6.5.2 in doubles, it touches first his right half-court and then, passing directly over or around the net assembly, touches the receiver's right half-court

3.6.6 When the ball is struck in service, it shall be behind the end line of the server's body, other than his arm, head or leg, which is farthest from the net.

3.6.7 It is the responsibility of the player to serve so that the umpire or assistant umpire can see that he complies with the requirements for a good service.
3.6.7.1 Except when an assistant umpire has been appointed the umpire may, on the first occasion in a match at which he has a doubt about the correctness of a player's service, interrupt play and warn the server without awarding a point.
3.6.7.2 On any subsequent occasion in the same match at which the same player's service action is of doubtful correctness, for the same or for any other reason, the player shall not be giventhe benefit of the doubt and shall lose a point.
3.6.7.3 Whenever there is a clear failure by the server to comply with the requirements for a good service no warning shall be given and he shall lose a point, on the first as on any other occasion.

3.6.8 Exceptionally, strict observance of any particular requirement for a good service may be waived where the umpire is notified, before play begins, that compliance with that requirement is prevented by physical disability.

3.7 A Good Return
3.7.1 The ball, having been served or returned, shall be struck so that it passes over or around the net assembly and touches the opponent's court, either directly, or after touching the net assembly.

3.8 The Order of Play
3.8.1 In singles, the server shall first make a good service , the receiver shall then make a good return and thereafter server and receiver alternately shall each make a good return.

3.8.2 In doubles, the server shall first make a good service, the receiver shall then make a good return, the partner of the server shall then make a good return, the partner of the receiver shall then make a good return and thereafter each player in turn in that sequence shall make a good return.

3.9 In Play
3.9.1 The ball shall be in play from the last moment at which it is stationary before being projected in service until
3.9.1.1 it touches anything other than the playing surface, the net assembly, the racket held in the hand or the racket hand below the wrist, or

3.9.1.2 the rally is otherwise decided as a let or a point.

3.10 A Let
3.10.1 The rally shall be a let
3.10.1.1 if in service the ball, in passing over or around the net assembly, touches it, provided the service is otherwise good or the ball is volleyed or obstructed by the receiver or his partner;
3.10.1.2 if the service is delivered when, in the opinion of the umpire, the receiving player or pair is not ready, provided that neither the receiver nor his partner attempts to strike the ball;
3.10.1.3 if, in the opinion of the umpire, failure to make a good service or otherwise to comply with the Laws is due to a disturbance outside the control of the player;
3.10.1.4 if it is interrupted to correct an error in the order of service, receiving or ends;
3.10.1.5 if it is interrupted to introduce the expedite system;
3.10.1.6 if it is interrupted to warn a player that his service is of doubtful correctness or that he has failed to notify a change of racket;
3.10.1.7 if the conditions of play are disturbed in a way which, in the opinion of the umpire, is likely to affect the outcome of the rally.

3.11 A Point
3.11.1 Unless the rally is a let, a player shall lose a point
3.11.1.1. if he fails to make a good service;
3.11.1.2 if he fails to make a good return;
3.11.1.3 if he volleys or obstructs the

ball, except as provided in 3.10.1.1;
3.11.1.4 if he strikes the ball twice successively;
3.11.1.5 if the ball touches his court twice successively;
3.11.1.6 if he strikes the ball with a side of the racket blade whose surface does not comply with the requirements of 3.4.2;
3.11.1.7 if he, or anything he wears or carries, moves the playing surface while the ball is in play;
3.11.1.8 if his free hand touches the playing surface while the ball is in play;
3.11.1.9 if he, or anything he wears or carries, touches the net assembly while the ball is in play;
3.11.1.10 if, as he serves, he or his partner stamps his foot;
3.11.1.11 if, in doubles, he strikes the ball out of the sequence established by the server and receiver;
3.11.1.12 if, under the expedite system, he serves and the receiving player or pair makes thirteen successive good returns.

3.12 A Game
3.12.1 A game shall be won by the player or pair first scoring 21 points unless both players or pairs score 20 points, when the game shall be won by the player or pair first scoring subsequently 2 points more than the opposing player or pair.

3.13 A Match
3.13.1 A match shall consist of the best of three games or the best of five games.
3.13.2 Play shall be continuous throughout a match except that any player shall be entitled to claim an

interval of not more than two minutes between successive games.

3.14 The Choice of Serving, Receiving and Ends
3.14.1 The right to make first choice shall be decided by lot.
3.14.2 The player or pair winning this right may
3.14.2.1 choose to serve or receive first, when the loser shall have the choice of ends;
3.14.2.2 choose an end, when the loser shall have the choice of serving or receiving first;
3.14.2.3 require the loser to make the first choice, when the winner shall have whichever choice is not made by the loser.

3.14.3 In doubles, the pair having the right to serve first in each game shall decide which of them will do so and
3.14.3.1 in the first game of a match, the opposing pair shall then decide which of them will receive first;
3.14.3.2 in subsequent games of the match, the first receiver will be determined by the choice of server, as provided in 3.15.5.

3.15 The Order of Serving, Receiving and Ends
3.15.1 After 5 points have been scored the receiving player or pair shall become the serving player or pair and so on until the end of the game, or until each player or pair has scored 20 points or until the introduction of the expedite system.

3.15.2 In doubles,
3.15.2.1 the first server shall be the selected player of the pair having the

right to serve first and the first receiver shall be the appropriate player of the opposing pair;
3.15.2.2 the second server shall be the player who was the first receiver and the second receiver shall be the partner of the first receiver;
]3.15.2.3 the third server shall be the partner of the first server and the third receiver will be the partner of the first receiver;
13.15.2.4 the fourth server shall be the partner of the first receiver and the fourth receiver shall be the first server;
3.15.2.5 the fifth server shall be the player who was the first server and the players shall thereafter serve in the same sequence until the end of the game.

3.15.3 If both players or pairs have scored 20 points or if the expedite system is in operation the sequence of serving and receiving shall be the same but each player shall serve for only one point in turn until the end of the game

3.15.4 The player or pair who served first in a game shall receive first in the immediately subsequent game of the match.

3.15.5 In each game of a doubles match after the first, the first server having been chosen, the first receiver shall be the player who served to him in the immediately preceding game.

3.15.6 In the last possible game of a doubles match the pair due next to receive shall change the order of

receiving when first either pair scores 10 points.

3.15.7 The player or pair starting at one end in a game shall start at the other end in the immediately subsequent game of the match.

3.15.8 In the last possible game of a match the players shall change ends when first either player or pair scores 10 points.

3.16 Out of Order of Serving, Receiving and Ends
3.16.1 If a player serves or receives out of turn, play shall be interrupted by the umpire as soon as the error is discovered and shall resume with those players serving and receiving who should be server and receiver respectively at the score that has been reached, according to the sequence established at the beginning of the match and, in doubles, to the order of serving chosen by the pair having the right to serve first in the game during which the error is discovered.

3.16.2 If the players have not changed ends when they should have done so, play shall be interrupted by the umpire as soon as the error is discovered and shall resume with the players at the ends at which they should be at the score that has been reached, according to the sequence established at the beginning of the match.

3.16.3 In any circumstances, all points scored before the discovery of an error shall be reckoned.

3.17 The Expedite System

3 17.1 The expedite system shall come into operation if a game is unfinished after fifteen minutes' play, or at any earlier time at the request of both players or pairs.

3.17.1.1 If the ball is in play when the time limit is reached, play shall be interrupted by the umpire and shall resume with service by the player who served in the rally that was interrupted.

3.17.1.2 If the ball is not in play when the time limit is reached, play shall resume with service by the player who received in the immediately preceding rally of the game

3.17.2 Thereafter, each player shall serve for one point in turn, in accordance with 3.15.3, and if the rally is not decided before the receiving player or pair makes thirteen good returns the server shall not lose a point.

3.17.3 Once introduced, the expedite system shall remain in operation for the remainder of the match.

Chapter 4
Regulations for International Competitions

4.1 Scope of Laws and Regulations
4.1. Types of Competition

4.1.1.1 An 'international competition' is a competition which may include the players of more than one Association.

4.1.1.2 'World Championships' are the World Championship title competitions organized by an Association authorized by the ITTF to do so.

4.1.1.3 'Continental Championships' are the Continental championship title competitions organized by a Continental Federation and recognised by the ITTF.

4.1.1.4 'Open International Championships' are the Association championship title competitions organized by an Association and recognized by the ITTF.

4.1.1.5 An 'international match' is a match between teams representing Associations.

4.1.1.6 An 'open tournament' is a tournament which is open for entry to the players of all Associations

4.1.1.7 A 'restricted tournament' is a tournament which is restricted for entry to specified groups of players, other than age groups.

4.1.1.8 An 'invitation tournament' is a tournament which is restricted for entry to individual players , individually invited.

4.1.2 Applicability

4.1.2.1 The Laws (Chapter 3) shall apply to the World, Continental and Open International Championships, Open Tournaments and, unless otherwise agreed by the participating Associations, to international matches.

4.1.2.2 The Laws are recommended for all other international competitions and Associations are recommended to adopt the Laws for their domestic competitions.

4.1.2.3 The Regulations for International competitions shall apply, subject to any limitation specified in a particular Regulation, to:

4.1.2.3.1 World Championships, World Cup Tournaments and World Grand Prix tournaments unless otherwise authorized by the Council and notified in advance to the participating Associations;

4.1.2.3.2 Continental Championships, unless otherwise authorized by the appropriate Continental Federation and notified in advance to the participating Associations;

4.1.2.3.3 Open International Championships, unless otherwise authorized by the ITTF and agreed by the participants in accordance with 4.1.2.4;

4.1.2.3.4 other open tournaments, unless otherwise agreed by the participants in accordance with 4.1.2.4;

RULES OF THE GAME

4.1.2.3.5 international matches, unless otherwise agreed by the participating Associations.

4.1.2.4 Where an open tournament does not comply with a Regulation the nature and extent of the variation shall be specified in the entry form; completion and submission of an entry form shall be regarded as signifying agreement by the entrant to the conditions of the competition, including such variations.

4.1.2.5 These regulations are recommended for all other international competitions but, provided that the Constitution and Disciplinary Regulations are observed:
4.1.2.5.1 regional competitions other than Continental Championships may be held under rules laid down from time to time by the appropriate regional authority;
4.1.2.5.2 international restricted and invitation tournaments and recognised international competitions organized by unaffiliated bodies may be held under rules laid down by the organizing authority or mutually agreed;
4.1.2.5.3 competitions restricted to the players of one Association may be held under rules laid down by that Association.

4.1.2.6 In general, the Laws and the Regulations for International Competitions shall be [resumed to apply unless variations have been agreed in advance or are made clear in the published rules of the competition.

4.2 Equipment and Playing Conditions
4.2.1 Playing equipment
4.2.1.1 In World, Continental and Open International Championships
4.2.1.1.1 the table, the net and the ball shall each be of a brand and type currently approved by the ITTF;
4.2.1.1.2 the covering material on a side of the blade used for striking the ball shall be of a brand and type currently authorized by the ITTF;
4.2.1.1.3 the surface of one side of the racket shall be bright red and the surface of the other side shall be black, whether or not both sides are used for striking the ball.

4.2.1.2 The approval and authorization of playing equipment shall be conducted in accordance with directives agreed by the Council.
4.2.1.3 It is the responsibility of the player to ensure that the racket he uses can be seen to comply with the requirements of the relevant Laws and Regulations.

4.2.2 Clothing
4.2.2.1 Playing clothing shall normally consist of a short-sleeved shirt and shorts or skirt, socks and playing shoes; other garments, such as part or all of a track suit, shall not be worn during play except with the permission of the referee.

4.2.2.2 A playing shirt, shorts or skirt shall be mainly of a uniform colour other than white, but
4.2.2.2.1 the collar and sleeves of a playing shirt may be of a contrasting colour or colours other than white;
4.2.2.2.2 the background colour may include narrow stripes, in one direction only and of contrasting colour other than white, having a width not greater than 1mm and a spacing of not less than 30mm;
4.2.2.2.3 trimming of white or any colour, contained within a total width of 10mm, may be used along the edges and side seams of a garment

4.2.2.3 A playing garment may carry
4.2.2.3.1 a badge or lettering on the front or side contained within a total area of 64sq cm;
4.2.2.3.2 numbers or lettering on the back of a playing shirt to identify a player, his Association or, in club matches, his club;
4.2.2.3.3 advertisements in accordance with the provisions of 4.2..4.6;
4.2.2.3.4 the ITTF logo, where the design has been authorized by the ITTF.

4.2.2.4 Any markings or trimming on the front or side of a playing garment and any objects such as jewellery worn by a player shall not be so conspicuous or brightly reflecting as to unsight an opponent.

4.2.2.5 Any question of the legality or acceptability of playing clothing shall be decided by the referee, except that he may not rule illegal or unacceptable a design which has been authorized by the ITTF.

4.2.2.6 In World and Continental Championships the players of a team taking part in a team match, and players from the same Association forming a doubles pair, shall be dressed uniformly, with the possible exception of socks and shoes.

4.2.2.7 In World and Continental Championships, it is recommended that opposing players and pairs wear clothing that is sufficiently different to enable them to be easily distinguished by spectators.

4.2.2.7.1 Where both players or pairs normally wear clothing of the same colour or colours, they should be asked to agree which player or pair will change either shirt or shorts, or both, for garments of a different colour.

4.2.2.7.2 If the players or pairs are unable to agree which will change, the choice should be made by lot.

4.2.3 Playing conditions

4.2.3.1 The playing space shall not be less than 14m long, 7m wide and 4m high.

4.2.3.2 The playing area shall be enclosed by dark coloured surrounds about 75cm high, separating it from adjacent playing areas and from spectators.

4.2.3.3 The light intensity, measured at the height of the playing surface, shall not be less than 400 lux uniformly over the whole of the playing surface and the intensity at any other part of the playing area shall not be less than half the intensity over the playing surface.

4.2.3.4 The light source shall not be less than 4m above the floor.

4.3.3.5 The background shall be generally dark and shall not contain bright light sources nor daylight through uncovered windows or other apertures.

4.2.3.6 The floor shall not be light-coloured nor brightly reflecting and its surface shall not be of brick, concrete or stone.

4.2.4 Advertisements

4.2.4.1 Inside the playing area advertisements shall be displayed only on equipment or fittings which are normally present and there shall be no special additional displays.

4.2.4.2 Fluorescent or luminescent colours shall not be used anywhere within the playing area and white shall not be used on the inside of surrounds.

4.2.4.3 Lettering or symbols on the inside of surrounds shall be contained within a total height of 40cm.

4.1.4.4 Advertisements on tables shall be only on the longer sides of the table top and not on the legs or supporting structure, and shall be limited to the maker's normal trademark, symbol or name contained within a total area on any face of 200 sq cm.

4.2.4.5 Advertisements on umpire's tables or other furniture inside the playing area shall be contained within a total area on any face of 750 sq cm.

4.2.4.6 Advertisements on players' clothing , other than on players'

numbers, shall not be white and shall be limited to

4.2.4.6.1 the maker's normal trademark, symbol or name contained within a total area of 24 sq cm;

4.2.4.6.2 not more than two advertisements, each contained within a total area of 40 sq cm and clearly separated from each other, on the front or side of a shirt ;

4.2.4.6.3 one advertisement, contained within a total area of 40 sq cm, on shorts or skirt;

4.2.4.6.4 one advertisement, contained within a total area of 200 sq cm, on the back of a shirt.

4.2.4.7 Advertisements on players' numbers shall be contained within a total area of 100 sq cm

4.2.4.8 At World Championships, advertisements within the playing area other than for table tennis equipment shall be permitted only with the approval of the Council or of the Executive Committee acting on behalf of the Council.

4.3 Jurisdiction of Officials
4.3.1 Referee

4.3.1.1 For each competition as a whole a responsible referee shall be appointed and his identity and location shall be made known to the participants and, where appropriate, to the team captains.

4.3.1.2 The referee shall be responsible, in accordance with the relevant regulations, for

4.3.1.2.1 the conduct of the draw:

4.3.1.2.2 the scheduling of matches by time and table;

4.3.1.2.3 the appointment of match officials;

4.3.1.2.4 deciding any question of interpretation of Laws or Regulations, including the legality of clothing and other equipment;

4.3.1.2.5 deciding whether players may wear track suits during a match;

4.3.1.2.6 deciding whether play may be suspended in any emergency;

4.3.1.2.7 deciding whether players may leave the playing area during a match;

4.3.1.2.8 deciding whether statutory practice periods may be extended;

4.3.1.2.9 taking disciplinary action for misbehaviour or other breaches of regulations.

4.3.1.3 Where with agreement of the completion of the competition management committee, any of the duties of the referee are delegated to other persons, the specific responsibilities and locations of each of these persons shall be made known to the participants and, where appropriate, to the team captains.

4.3.1.4 The referee, or a responsible deputy appointed to exercise authority in his absence, shall be present at all times during play.

4.3.1.5 Where the referee is satisfied that it is desirable to do so he may replace an umpire or subsidiary match official at any time, but he may not alter any decision already made by the replaced official on a question of fact within his jurisdiction.

4.3.2 Match Officials

4.3.2.1 In World, Continental and Open International Championships an umpire and an assistant umpire shall be appointed for each individual match; in other competitions an assistant umpire may be appointed at the discretion of the referee.

4.3.2.2 If an assistant umpire is appointed he shall sit opposite the umpire, in line with the net, and shall:

4.3.2.2.1 monitor the duration of the practice period before the start of a match, of play during a game and of authorized intervals;

4.3.2.2.2 count the strokes of the receiving player or pair when the expedite system is in operation, except as provided in 4.3.2.3;

4.3.2.2.3 decide whether the ball in play touches the side of the table facing him, the top edge of the playing surface on that side, or neither;

4.3.2.2.4 decide whether a service is legal, as provided in 4.3.2.4

4.3.2.3 In World and Continental Championships, and where an assistant umpire is not appointed, a separate official shall be appointed to count strokes when the expedite system is in operation.

4.3.2.4 The decision of the umpire, assistant umpire stroke counter shall be final on any decision of fact within his jurisdiction except that, provided the action is clearly visible to him, either the umpire or the assistant umpire may decide that a player's service is illegal.

4.3.2.5 Where an assistant umpire is not appointed, the umpire shall assume his duties, except as provided in 4.3.2.3.

4.3.3 Appeals

4.3.3.1 No agreement between players, in an individual event, or between team captains, in a team event, can alter a decision on a question of interpretation of Laws or Regulations by the responsible referee or on any other question of tournament or match conduct by the responsible management committee.

4.3.3.2 No appeal may be made against a decision on a question of fact by the responsible match official or on a question of interpretation of Laws or Regulations, by the responsible referee.

4.3.3.3 An appeal may be made to the referee against a decision of a match official on a question of interpretation of Laws or Regulations, and the decision of the referee shall be final.

4.3.3.4 An appeal may be made to the competition management committee against a decision of a referee on a question of tournament or match conduct not covered by the Laws or Regulations, and the decision of the management committee shall be final.

4.3.3.5 In an individual event an appeal may be made only by a player participating in the match in which the question has arisen; in a team event an appeal may be made only by the captain of a team participating in the match in which the question has arisen.

4.3.3.6 A question of interpretation of

Laws or Regulations arising from the decision of a referee, or a question of tournament or match conduct arising from the decision of a competition management committee, may be submitted by the player or team captain eligible to make an appeal, through his parent Association, for consideration by the ITTF Rules Committee; the Rules Committee shall give a ruling as a guide for future decisions, and this ruling may also be made the subject of a protest by an Association to the Council or a General Meeting, but it shall not affect the finality of any decision already made by the responsible referee or management committee.

4.4 Match Conduct
4.4.1 Scoring
4.4.1.1 The umpire shall call the score immediately the ball is out of play at the completion of a rally, or as soon as is practicable thereafter taking into account of any applause or other noise which may prevent the call from being heard.
4.4.1.1.1 In calling the score during a game the umpire shall call first the number of points scored by the player or pair due to serve in the next rally of the game and then the number of points scored by the opposing player or pair.
4.4.1.1.2 At the beginning of a game and before any change of server the umpire shall follow the score call by naming the next server.
4.4.1.1.3 At the end of the game the umpire shall name the winning player or pair and shall then call the number of points scored by the winning player or pair followed by the number of

points scored by the losing player or pair.
4.4.1.1.4 When a rally is a let the umpire is recommended to repeat the previous score call before the next rally begins, to indicate that no point has been scored.

4.4.1.2 In addition to calling the score the umpire may use hand signals to indicate his decisions,
4.4.1.2.1 When a point has been scored, he may raise to shoulder level the hand nearer to the player or pair who won the point.
4.4.1.2.2 At the start of the game or at the change of service he may point with his hand towards the player or pair due to serve next.

4.4.1.3 The server is recommended not to serve until all the players are aware of the correct score, either through hearing the umpire's score call or by seeing the score indicators: if the server frequently serves prematurely and the umpire considers that this is adversely affecting an opponent, the umpire shall warn the server to delay his service and shall, if necessary, remind the receiver to indicate, by raising his free hand, that he is not ready.

4.4.1.4 The score shall be called in the language of the Association in whose territory the competition takes place or in any other language acceptable to both players or pairs and to the umpire.

4.4.1.5 The score shall be displayed on mechanical or electrical indicators so that it is clearly visible to the

players and, as far as is practicable, to the spectators;

4.4.1.6 When the umpire warns a player about a service of doubtful correctness he shall hold up a blue card which is visible to the players and spectators; a player may receive only one such warning during a match, for any reason.

4.4.2 Expedite Procedure
4.4.2.1 The duration of play in any game in which the expedite system is not already in operation shall be monitored by the assistant umpire.

4.4.2.2 The assistant umpire shall start the clock immediately the ball is first in play in each game and shall stop and re-start it for interruptions of play other than momentary breaks; such interruptions may be due to the ball going outside the playing area, the change of ends in the last possible game of a match, towelling, adjustment of clothing, replacement of damaged equipment or recovery from a fall or injury.

4.4.2.3 At the end of fifteen minutes play in any game in which the expedite system is not already in operation, the assistant umpire shall call 'time'; the umpire shall then call 'let', shall inform the players that the remainder of the match will be played under the expedite system and shall then re-start play, without any interval.

4.4.2.4 Thereafter, in each rally, the number of each stroke made by the receiving player or pair, from one to

thirteen, shall be called out so that it is clearly audible to the players
4.4.2.4.1 The call shall be made immediately after the ball is struck.
4.4.2.4.2 The number shall be called in English or in any other language acceptable to both players' or pairs and to the umpire.

4.4.2.5 If play continues after the thirteenth return the umpire shall call 'stop'.

4.4.3 Procedure for Assistant Umpire

4.4.3.1 If the assistant umpire is sure that a player's service action is illegal he shall call 'fault' and the umpire shall award the point against the server; if he cannot be sure that a fault has been committed he shall take no action.

4.4.3.2 If the assistant umpire is sure that the ball in play strikes the side of the table facing him he shall call 'side' an the umpire shall award a point against the player who last struck the ball.

4.4.3.3. It is recommended that, after making the appropriate call, the assistant umpire raise his hand above his head to draw attention to the action he has taken.

4.4.4. Continuity of Play

4.4.4.1 It is the duty of the umpire to ensure that play throughout a match is continuous, except during any authorized intervals.
4.4.4.1.1 He may allow the shortest reasonable pauses for such purposes as towelling, but only after every five points; towels should be kept near the umpire,
4.4.4.1.2 He shall not allow these pauses to be prolonged by conversation or lingering and whenever either player or pair is ready to continue the other player or pair should be called on to do so.

4.4.4.2 If a player breaks his racket during play he shall replace it immediately with either another racket which he has brought with him to the playing area or one which is handed to him in the playing area.

4.4.4.3 If a match cannot proceed because the players are unable to agree on the choice of a ball the umpire shall choose one at random; a player refusing to accept this choice may be disqualified by the referee. It is recommended that wherever practicable, players should be asked to check proposed match balls before they go to the match table and to choose two or three which are mutually acceptable.

4.4.4.4. The referee may allow a suspension of play, of the shortest practical duration, if a player is temporarily incapacitated by an accident, provided that in the opinion of the referee the suspension is not likely to be unduly disadvantageous to the opposing player or pair.

4.4.4.5 A suspension shall not be allowed for a disability which was present or was reasonably to be expected at the beginning of the match, or where it is due to the normal stress of play; disability such as cramp or exhaustion, caused by the player's current state of fitness or by the manner in which play has proceeded does not justify such an emergency suspension, which may be allowed only for incapacity resulting from an accident, such as injury caused by a fall.

4.4.4.6 Players shall remain in or near the playing area throughout a match, except with the permission of the referee; during authorized intervals between games they shall remain within three metres of the playing area, under the supervision of the umpire.

4.4.5 Practice

4.4.5.1 Players are entitled to practise on the match table for up to two minutes immediately before the start of a match; the specified practice period may be extended only with the permission of the referee

4.4.5.2 Players shall be given reasonable opportunity to check and to familiarize themselves with any equipment which they are to use, but they shall not automatically entitle them to more than a few practice rallies before resuming play after the replacement of a damaged ball or racket.

4.4.5.3 Players shall not practise on the match table during the intervals between games or during any other authorized suspension of play; during an emergency suspension the referee may, at his discretion, allow players to practise on any table.

4.4.6 Advice to Players

4.4.6.1 A player may receive advice from anyone during the intervals between games or during any other authorized suspension of play but he shall not receive advice at any other time in a match.

4.4.6.2 The purpose of this restriction is to prevent distracting interruptions and to place upon the player responsibility for his own strategy and tactics during a game.

4.4.6.2.1 Association and match officials shall discourage attempts to give or to receive advice other than at the authorized times or otherwise to influence play while it is in progress

4.4.6.2.2 If such attempts persist after a warning by the umpire he shall ask the adviser to leave the vicinity of the playing area for the remainder of the match that is in progress; if the adviser refuses to leave the umpire should suspend play and report immediately to the referee.

4.4.6.3 This restriction applies only to advice on play and nothing in these regulations shall prevent a player or captain, as appropriate, from making a formal appeal against the decision of a match official or hinder a consultation between a player and his Association representative or interpreter on the explanation of a juridicial decision.

4.4.7 Behaviour of Players

4.4.7.1 Umpires and captains shall discourage players from mannerisms or behaviour that may unfairly affect an opponent, may offend spectators or may bring the game into disrepute.

4.4.7.2 When the umpire considers that, for any of these reasons, the conduct of a player in the playing area is not of an acceptable standard he shall warn the player and ask him to refrain from the offending behaviour.

4.4.7.3 The referee may, at his discretion, take disciplinary action against a player for persistent unfair or offensive behaviour, whether reported by the umpire or not; such action may include disqualification from an event or from a whole competition.

4.4.7.4 If a player fails to notify the umpire and his opponent when he changes his racket during a match the umpire shall immediately report the matter to the referee; on the first occasion the referee shall warn the player and on any subsequent occasion the referee shall disqualify him.

4.4.8 Doping

4.4.8.1 There shall be no doping before or during play in any competition.

4.4.8.2 For the purpose of these regulations, doping is the introduction into the body in any way of a list of prohibited substances with the object of improving performance during competition.

4.4.8.3 At World Championships, anti-doping controls shall be carried out in accordance with directives issued by the Council.

4.4.8.3.1 These directives, which shall be based on medical advice , shall include details of the procedure for the conduct of tests and of the imposition of penalties.

4.4.8.3.2 Any directives authorized by the Council under these regulations shall be issued to all Associations not later than six calendar months before the start of the championships to which they are to apply.

4.4.9 Betting

4.4.9.1 There shall be no betting of any kind on players or matches.

THIS BOOK HAS SHOWN THE IMPORTANCE AND WIDE-RANGING ROLE OF THE COACH. IT HAS ALSO INDICATED THE KNOWLEDGE REQUIRED TO BE AN EFFECTIVE AND SUCCESSFUL COACH. THE SCOPE OF THIS BOOK CANNOT COVER EVERY ASPECT IN DETAIL, SO IF YOU HAVE DEVELOPED AN INTEREST IN SOME ASPECT OF COACHING SUCH AS MENTAL PREPARATION, FITNESS TRAINING OR THE PREVENTION OF INJURY, **THE NATIONAL COACHING FOUNDATION**, ESTABLISHED TO PROVIDE A SERVICE FOR SPORTS COACHES, RUNS COURSES, PRODUCES STUDY PACKS, BOOKS, VIDEOS AND OTHER RESOURCES ON MANY PERFORMANCE-RELATED AREAS PARTICULARLY DESIGNED FOR THE PRACTISING COACH.

CONTACT **THE NATIONAL COACHING FOUNDATION** AT: 4 COLLEGE CLOSE, BECKETT PARK, LEEDS LS6 3QH. TELEPHONE: LEEDS (0532) 744802

DATE D

26 APR
-1 SEP
-6 OCT
5 MAY
2 0 JU05

NOVA Library Products